꒜꒜꒜꒜꒜꒜꒜꒜

The Future of
Student Affairs

*A Guide to Student Development
for Tomorrow's Higher Education*

Theodore K. Miller
Judith S. Prince

The Future of
Student Affairs

Jossey-Bass Publishers

San Francisco • London • 1988

THE FUTURE OF STUDENT AFFAIRS
A Guide to Student Development for Tomorrow's Higher Education
by Theodore K. Miller and Judith S. Prince

Copyright © 1976 by: Jossey-Bass Inc., Publishers
350 Sansome Street
San Francisco, California 94104
&
Jossey-Bass Limited
28 Banner Street
London EC1Y 8QE

Library of Congress Catalogue Card Number LC 76-19496

International Standard Book Number ISBN 0-87589-298-1

Manufactured in the United States of America

JACKET DESIGN BY WILLI BAUM
FIRST EDITION
First printing: December 1976
Second printing: March 1977
Third printing: November 1977
Fourth printing: March 1984
Fifth printing: November 1988

Code 7621

This publication is sponsored by

THE AMERICAN COLLEGE PERSONNEL ASSOCIATION

ᚼᚼᚼᚼᚼᚼᚼ

Foreword

The American College Personnel Association (ACPA) is pleased
to present *The Future of Student Affairs* to the higher education community. It is the culmination of the second phase of
the Association's Tomorrow's Higher Education Project (T.H.E.),
an activity initiated eight years ago for the purpose of examining
the future of college student personnel work.

Phase one produced, in 1972, a monograph by Robert D.
Brown titled *Student Development in Tomorrow's Higher Education: A Return to the Academy.* That monograph sets forth a view
of the fundamental goals and premises of higher education, provides
an analysis and synthesis of the literature that projects the probable
future of higher education, and suggests the need for greater integration of academic and student affairs.

Since 1972, ACPA has explored a new conceptual model for
the practice of student personnel work in the future. It has solicited
reaction and recommendations from members regarding higher
education programs that are currently implementing one or more
aspects of the model. It now shares the report of these activities in
this publication.

Foreword

ACPA is grateful to both Theodore K. Miller and Judith S. Prince for taking on the responsibilities of writing this document. Theodore Miller has served the Association and this project in many ways. Under his able leadership as ACPA president in 1975–76, the development of skill-building activities designed to help practitioners to incorporate the competencies described herein was begun. Judith Prince was the able chairperson for the Project during the phase that is now ending.

The Association wishes to recognize those who served on the task force that gave the project its birth, including Russell Brown, W. Harold Grant, Donald Hoyt, Jane Matson, Albert Miles, Philip Tripp, and Dyckman Vermilye, with Donald Kubit as coordinator. The second phase of their goal has now been completed. The Association is also appreciative of the countless others who have contributed to the development of this project.

ACPA hopes that the publication of this book will help to energize and focus the forces that are attempting to individualize higher education. It acknowledges the need for continual reexamination and reconceptualization of the nature of student development and student personnel work in an ever-changing educational and societal context. The effort to individualize higher education has long been in the making. Although its pace has been uneven and unpredictable, its direction is clear and its advance is unmistakable. The Tomorrow's Higher Education Project is one of the significant and viable ways to continue this effort.

The activities of ACPA in this arena will continue. A project has already been begun that is designed to identify, and subsequently to assess, the skills and competencies student personnel staffs will need in order to foster student development. ACPA will encourage activities designed to experiment with its recommendations and will welcome reaction. It will continue to monitor activities in all kinds of higher education settings so that it can arrive at an ordered understanding of the nature of student development and the ways in which institutions of higher education can more adequately affect it.

October 26, 1976   Anne S. Pruitt, President
American College Personnel Association

❀❀❀❀❀❀❀

Preface

"We are . . . interested primarily in improving the quality of American higher education. We are convinced that the knowledge of human development from the behavioral sciences now makes possible a wider vision of what the school can accomplish and of more effective ways of teaching. American higher education has not paid enough attention to human development as a part of its mission, and the time has come for this neglect to end—*in the name of better education.*"

Nearly a decade has passed since the Committee on the Student in Higher Education issued the foregoing statement in 1968 under the auspices of the Hazen Foundation. These years have seen many changes in higher education. Some of them exhibit a new enlightenment among educational leaders, who are incorporating human development in the missions of their institutions. Others, however, are making retrenchment moves to preserve the status quo. Although the latter are understandable enough, they fail to recognize that higher education, like other social institutions, is constantly evolving as a dynamic human enterprise. It is essential, therefore, that educational leaders look to the needs of the American people, both now and in the future, when shaping their educational programs and approaches. Because we believe these needs go beyond intellectual growth, this book is dedicated to those who are seeking better ways to encourage the complete development of all human beings in their institutional environments.

Although we think student development is the responsibility of the full academic community, this book is concerned primarily with the role of student affairs practitioners and administrators. This focus is not meant in any way to reduce the importance of involvement and collaboration by all participants in the educational enterprise. In fact, we earnestly hope that all members of the college community will seriously consider our proposals, for no one person or group can accomplish the educational mission alone, including the student affairs staff. Together, however, through cooperation and integrated programming, more effective education of the whole person is possible.

This book has two primary purposes. The first is to provide the basic theories and principles of a useful approach to integrating human developmental concepts in higher education. The second is to describe specific strategies that can be used by those who wish to apply the model on their own campuses. We are well aware of the fact that this book does not definitively resolve the many problems facing student affairs professionals who wish to introduce new and better developmental programs. In many ways, it raises more questions than it answers. Nevertheless, it provides the reader with an introduction to many important components along with referrals to numerous resources which can be used to obtain a deeper understanding of the somewhat complex and multifaceted model being presented. As an additional resource, numerous examples of student

Preface

development programs which have been submitted by colleagues throughout the country are presented to reveal the many forms this approach can take, depending on the unique needs and characteristics of a given institution and its students. Unfortunately, space limitations did not permit inclusion of every program submitted. The addendum following Chapter Nine, however, identifies individuals who may be contacted regarding various developmental program approaches. We realize, also, that this attempt to bridge human development theory and student development practice is not completed with the publication of this book. We believe, nevertheless, that the alternatives proposed will help to construct more and better bridges in the future.

This book represents several years of deliberation and task force activity by members of the American College Personnel Association (ACPA) and others concerned with bettering higher education. Basically, the model described here extends ideas put forward in 1938, and revised in 1949, by the American Council on Education's Committee on Student Personnel Work and published as the *Student Personnel Point of View*. It also reflects the endeavors of the Commission on Professional Development of the Council of Student Personnel Associations (COSPA) in Higher Education, whose statement entitled "Student Development Services in Higher Education" was completed in 1972 before the dissolution of the Council.

More specifically, the book is a direct result of work begun in 1968 when the ACPA president, Donald Hoyt, appointed a group to develop a strategy for examining the future of college student personnel work. In subsequent years association presidents Charles L. Lewis, Paul A. Bloland, William R. Butler, G. Robert Ross, Merrill C. Beyerl, and W. Harold Grant continued in their own ways to direct what became known as the Tomorrow's Higher Education (T.H.E.) project. The initial product of the T.H.E. Project was Robert D. Brown's monograph entitled *Student Development in Tomorrow's Higher Education: A Return to the Academy*. This white paper was designed to initiate the essential dialogue that would lead to the subsequent model-building and implementation phases of the T.H.E. Project and focused primarily on defining the nature of learning and identifying the fundamental goals and premises of higher education. Then in June 1974 an invitational student development model-building conference was called by President Harold Grant. It is on the consensual determinations of that conference, held at the University of Georgia, that much of this presentation is based. The conference participants were: John Blackburn, University of Denver; Robert D. Brown, University of Nebraska; Richard B. Caple, University of Missouri; Everett M. Chandler, California Polytechnic State University; Donald G. Creamer, El Centro College; Burns B. Crookston, University of Connecticut; K. Patricia Cross, Educational Testing Service; W. Harold Grant, Auburn University; Melvene D. Hardee, Florida State University; and Theodore K. Miller, University of Georgia, chairperson. In addition, a process team of University of Georgia students and staff members worked with the conference participants. Its members were Roger G. Bryant, Kenneth L. Ender, Barry L. Jackson, Martha C. McBride, Fred B. Newton, and Judith S. Prince, process team chairperson. The first report of this conference, which sketched the student development model presented in this book, was published under the title "A Student Development Model for Student Affairs in Tomorrow's Higher Education" in the July 1975 issue of the *Journal of College Student Personnel.*

The chapter concerned with organizational development has incorporated thinking and materials derived from a second invitational conference, held in February 1976, for the purpose of further exploring the organizational issues with which one must deal when attempting to implement the model. Participants at this conference in Overland Park, Kansas, included: Maureen Connors, Case Western Reserve University; Robert Conyne, Illinois State University; Donald G. Creamer, El Centro College; John P. Donohue, Oakton Community College; W. Harold Grant, Auburn University; J. Eugene Knott, University of Rhode Island; Thomas Leemon, Columbia University; Stephan Lenton, Virginia Commonwealth University; Theodore K. Miller, University of Georgia; Clyde A. Parker, University of Minnesota; Anne S. Pruitt, Case Western Reserve University; Celestine Schall, Alverno College;

Preface

Walter Shaw, University of Denver; and Robert G. Schmalfeld, Oklahoma State University, chairperson. A process team also worked with these resource persons. The team members were Kenneth L. Ender, University of Georgia; Thomas M. Keys, Oklahoma State University; Randall L. Whittaker, Oklahoma State University; and Jo F. Dorris, Oklahoma State University, process team chairperson. The chapter is an earnest attempt to accurately interpret the thinking of these many people in their work, and we gratefully acknowledge their important contributions.

In addition to those who participated as resource people in the model-building conferences, we are indebted to numerous others who have aided the development of this book. Everett M. Chandler, Janet D. Greenwood, Gary R. Hanson, Charles Hartness, Jr., and Roger B. Winston, Jr., were most helpful as reviewers of various chapters, as was Philip Tripp who has given the T.H.E. Project his continued support and inspiration since its inception. And we have a special debt to the many student affairs practitioners who submitted outlines of student development programs being implemented on their own campuses for inclusion as examples. Also we are indebted to Carol Eriksen, our diligent copy editor, as well as to Dolores Lapinski and Becky Eash, who handled the typing chores. Without the support and direct assistance of all the people involved over the past several years, this document would never have been written. Likewise, without the continued support and professional good will of the ACPA leadership, represented by the Executive Council's consistent forward-thinking actions over the years, this project could not have been accomplished.

October 1976

Theodore K. Miller
Athens, Georgia

Judith S. Prince
Macon, Georgia

Contents

Contents

The Future of
Student Affairs

*A Guide to Student Development
for Tomorrow's Higher Education*

Chapter 1

❧❧❧❧❧❧❧❧

Rationale

No doubt the statement that "nothing is permanent but change itself" seems trite these days, but trite sayings often achieve that status because they are basically true. Though all of us sometimes wish we could stop the world and get off, none of us can escape for long from our obligations to participate in the continual re-creation of our society. To do so, individuals and institutions alike must frequently evaluate their roles within the larger community. Colleges and universities, in particular, must not only join in this process but lead it, because they have a unique capacity for marshaling society's intellectual forces.

The Future of Student Affairs

Change has always been a characteristic of higher education in this country. As the United States evolved from an agrarian colonial outpost to a complex postindustrial nation, postsecondary education likewise shifted from an elitist to an egalitarian system designed to develop a broadly enlightened citizenry. In recent years the need for renewal has generated many new forms: community colleges, cluster colleges, universities without walls, campus-free colleges, credit by examination, continuing education units, external degree programs, off-campus experiential learning plans, study abroad programs, upward bound programs, and competency-based education. An important impetus for this reformation is a concern for the total development of students. Over the years student personnel programs have done a great deal to help students make the most of their formal education. But very often both faculty members and learners have considered these programs to be just supplements or complements to regular instruction. Because these views stress teaching and research while giving "out-of-class" education a secondary status, they are dysfunctional. The full potential of students will not be developed until the emotional and physical aspects of their growth are given as much attention as the cognitive dimension. The informal curriculum of student affairs programs deserves coordinate status with formal instruction, since out-of-class educational experiences not only promote nonintellectual development but act as a catalyst for integrating the cognitive, affective, and psychomotor objectives of postsecondary education.

Student affairs professionals, in collaboration with teachers and students, can effectively improve the quality of college life; in fact, it is their responsibility to do so. Unfortunately, however, the profession has tended to react instead of take positive action. If student affairs workers are to influence what is to come, they must anticipate change, not merely adjust to it. For this purpose, a statement of the profession's aims, as well as an operational model of its responsibilities, is essential.

As Bruner (1971) has stated, "Reform of curriculum is not enough. Reform of the school is probably not enough. The issue is one of man's capacity for creating a culture, society, and technology

2

that not only feed him but keep him caring and belonging." This book will show how student affairs work can be reconceptualized and practical so that it helps to develop human beings who do care and who belong in the years ahead.

DEFINITIONS

In the interest of avoiding confusion, the nomenclature proposed by Crookston (1976) has been adopted. Since the term *Student personnel work* is somewhat anachronistic, it is used only to refer to past services and activities which focused on controlling the lives of students outside the classroom, laboratory, and library. *Student affairs* refers to a major administrative subdivision, like academic affairs and business affairs. The *student affairs practitioner, worker,* or *professional* is a staff member who carries out the responsibilities of this subdivision, including such functions as counseling, career planning and placement, housing, and coordinating student activities. The *student development educator* is a faculty member, student affairs professional, or any other person who purposefully works to bring about the growth of all engaged in higher education.

And what about *student development* itself, the heart of our enterprise? Obviously, at the most basic level, this term simply means the development of the whole college-going human being. But here it is defined more specifically as *the application of human development concepts in postsecondary settings so that everyone involved can master increasingly complex developmental tasks, achieve self-direction, and become interdependent.* It is, then, both a philosophical goal and the means for achieving it.

This is a grand and glorious aim, of course, and may seem rather familiar. Does student development as defined here differ from what faculty members have been doing in the classroom and what student affairs workers have been providing for years? The answer is that the philosophy has been with us for some time but has seldom been fully realized in practice.

A comprehensive review of the goals of higher education

3

since the first days of the University of Paris and the Sorbonne, undertaken by Brown (1972), revealed that "throughout history, almost without exception, the expressed or clearly implicit goals of colleges and universities have been to have an impact on students in ways more extensive than passing on facts, specific skills, or intellectual capacities" (p. 28). An important expression of these aims was given by the American Council on Education (ACE), first in 1938 and again in 1949 (Williamson). Four of the basic assumptions in its "Student Personnel Point of View" statement are the following: (1) the individual student must be considered as a whole; (2) each student is a unique person and must be treated as such; (3) the total environment of the student is educational and must be used to achieve his or her full development; (4) the major responsibility for a student's personal and social development rests with the student and his or her personal resources.

Although there are those who contend that what the individual student does of a personal, social, or political nature is not really the concern of an educational institution (Mayhew, 1968), the ACE "Point of View" implies that all kinds of nonintellectual learning should be part of a college's mission because they develop the whole student. To fulfill its mandate, an institution must act on the knowledge that each student arrives on campus with many developmental needs which must be met in a variety of ways, both formal and informal, and that no two students have the same requirements. But the college does not *prescribe* what the student shall learn. Rather, it provides resources and opportunities and helps students use them to best advantage.

Another influential proponent of the "whole person" philosophy is Sanford (1967), who advocates a broad general education to help students see their productive roles in perspective, develop values which can withstand organizational pressures, and lead meaningful lives apart from their occupations. By education for individual development, Sanford means a program consciously undertaken to promote an identity based on such qualities as flexibility, creativity, openness to experience, and responsibility (p. 9). Not limited to cognitive development alone, individual development represents, in part, an educational approach concerned with the emotional and

4

physical growth of students as well. Accomplishing this calls for bringing all campus resources into play in order to go beyond the traditional subject matter.

Despite the apparently broad implications of these views, the student development philosophy has usually been implemented only in separate and supplementary programs. These have come to be called "student services." Wrenn (1951) stated that "student personnel services and instructional services together form the educational program of the institution" (p. 27). And Cowley (1964) maintained that "these activities appear to me . . . to be complementary to the core teaching and research functions of colleges and universities. . . . The fact stands out clearly that the distinguishing characteristic of all members of all the groups in your fields is this: you serve students in various noncurricular ways" (p. 68).

Although many persons who work in the student affairs field would agree that educating all aspects of the human being is a worthy ideal, they have not usually quarreled with their separate and unequal role as educators. It is time to eliminate these differences. In the model being proposed, the development of the whole student is the mission and task of the whole college. Integration, equality, and collaboration are basic. The following expansions of the ACE principles are presented as the foundation of this student development approach.

• Human development is a continuous and cumulative process of physical, psychological, and social growth which can be divided into an orderly series of life stages. Each stage is characterized by certain developmental tasks that require the human to alter his or her present behavior and master new learning.

• Development is most likely to occur in an environment where change is anticipated, where individuals and groups work together to actively influence the future rather than just reacting to it after the fact.

• Systematic integration of cognitive, affective, and psychomotor experiences produces the most effective development.

• Several abilities and skills that facilitate growth in others have been identified; these can be learned, used, and taught by student development educators.

5

• The individual's development can be advanced by exposure to an organized problem-solving process that enables him or her to complete increasingly complex developmental tasks.

• Development is enhanced when students, faculty members, and student affairs practitioners work collaboratively to promote the continuous development of all.

THEORIES OF HUMAN DEVELOPMENT

The nature of human development is far from being completely known. Yet much important research and theorizing have been done in recent years, and educators should be familiar with them if they are to apply the concepts to their work with students.

Life Stages. A number of analysts have concluded from their observations that numerous developmental characteristics are relatively common to us all and that our growth seems to proceed in regular stages. Freud (1930), Tryon and Lilienthal (1950), Havighurst (1953), Piaget (1956), Maslow (1962), Blocher (1966), Perry (1970), Kohlberg and Turiel (1971) and others have described these stages in various ways. For instance, some authorities, such as Piaget and Kohlberg, conceptualize invariant developmental sequences for all individuals, while others, such as Erikson, Havighurst, and Maslow, postulate more general hierarchies, outlining developmental processes which individuals must go through if they are to continue growing. The many differences among these theoretical positions will not be examined here. What is important is their general agreement that until an individual has mastered the behavior characteristic of a given stage, he or she will have difficulty in successfully advancing to the next one.

A *stage* is a period of time when the individual is establishing new and varied behavior patterns and responses which differ from those at other periods. Movement through a particular stage, as through all of life, can best be described as a progression from simpler to more complex structures and activities. This principle of continuity is thus accompanied by that of cumulativeness. As individuals face life's challenges, they use their previous experiences and learning to help them develop ways of coping. So, at each successive stage, they integrate critical aspects of earlier stages in a more articu-

6

Rationale

late organization. Understanding this building process is important, for it offers a framework on which to establish both individualized assessment and intervention strategies. The ability to predict the probable developmental sequence and the approximate period when a given phase can be expected to occur is very useful. And the more we learn about the specific qualities of each step, the better our guidance of students will be. At the same time, it should be remembered that the stage is a rather arbitrary category and is not easily distinguished by casual observation, and individuals progress from one to the next at their own unique pace. Therefore, this theory should be looked at as an aid and as a framework for our observations and actions.

One of the earliest and best known stage sequences was proposed by Erikson (1959, 1963), who derived his eight stages of man (Table 1) from psychoanalytic theory and practice. Erikson postulated that individuals face a series of psychosocial crises as they attempt to cope with previously unencountered demands and circumstances. Because these crises arise from their interactions with their environment, the balance between their maturity level and society's expectations of persons at that level is important. Thus, the greater the discrepancy between the individual's present behavior and the degree of change that is expected by others, the greater the likelihood that a developmental disturbance will occur. The results of failing to meet each particular stage crisis are indicated in the Table as distrust, shame, guilt, and so on.

TABLE 1. Erikson's Eight Stages of Man

Stage	Nature of the Crisis
One: Oral-Sensory	Basic Trust v. Basic Distrust
Two: Muscular-Anal	Autonomy v. Shame and Doubt
Three: Ambulatory-Genital	Initiative v. Guilt
Four: Latency	Industry v. Inferiority
Five: Youth, Puberty and Adolescence	Identity v. Role Confusion
Six: Young Adulthood	Intimacy v. Isolation
Seven: Adulthood	Generativity v. Stagnation
Eight: Maturity	Ego Integrity v. Despair

7

The necessity of experiencing psychological crises in order to develop has been seriously challenged of late. King (1970), reporting on the ten-year Harvard Student Study, indicates that the developmental processes experienced by most students represented a model of continuity rather than crisis. This finding suggests that to expect a majority of human beings to express extreme personal turmoil and crisis when advanced development occurs is a somewhat erroneous idea which probably grew from clinical generalizations. Although the popular view has been that most individuals experience an identity crisis as part of their normal adolescence, for instance, the Harvard Student Study findings do not concur. This does not mean that psychosocial crisis is nonexistent, however. Rather, it suggests that many people grow without undergoing a great deal of disturbance. If the word *crisis* is attached to any critical juncture, decisive moment, or turning point when circumstances require the individual to alter present behavior or master new behavior, with or without undue trauma, then the term becomes somewhat less problematic. Sensitivity to the possibility of such crises is essential if truly relevant developmental programming is to be created.

The way people handle crises and the other aspects of their development is clearly influenced by their personal interests and cultural heritage. This does not mean that life stages differ among cultures, but does mean that the specific demands and manifest behavior may take different forms. And conversely, individual differences may bring about different specific demands within a given culture. For example, Coleman (1963) found that many career and life style options are open to young people, but once they make a particular choice, they must accept certain societal expectations associated with their choice. In effect, the social role an individual selects, or cannot escape from, has a potent effect on future development.

As people grow, they encounter an increasing number of these cultural expectations, which may relate to cognitive, affective, or psychomotor development. When they have no ready solution to a problem or come into conflict with new situations, tension and

8

anxiety usually result. But when they manage to meet the demands, thereby reducing anxiety, change occurs. This change, then, represents the basic unit in human development. A demand (challenge, crisis, need, task) is faced and overcome by changing one's behavior and by learning something new.

Developmental Tasks. In each life stage a person must deal with several relatively uniform developmental tasks; that is, he or she should acquire the skills, knowledge, functions, or attitudes which are appropriate for this period, according to the dictates of his or her physical maturation, social environment, and individual characteristics. This task concept, which was first used in print by Blos (1941), has been interpreted differently by various authorities, but it continues to be a useful tool for analyzing human development. One of the earliest descriptions was presented by Tryon and Lilienthal (1950), who divide the growth period into five stages—infancy, early and late childhood, and early and late adolescence. The successful completion of one set of tasks brings the individual to the threshold of a new series. Of the ten types of behavior and adjustment identified, eight culminate during late adolescence. These include achieving an appropriate balance between dependence and independence, learning to give and receive affection, relating to changing social groups, developing a conscience, learning one's psycho-socio-biological sex role, accepting and adjusting to a changing body, developing the necessary symbol system and conceptual abilities, and relating to the cosmos. Some of these tasks are concerned primarily with internal development, but most result from interactions with others. And all of them are represented in some form in the life stages which precede the one in which they are finally resolved. Probably each task is revealed in its purest form during the period when circumstances *force* the individual to resolve it. The relative difficulty of this resolution depends, then, on how well the person handled its antecedents. The upheaval, anxiety, or crisis that some individuals experience may well result from facing a task for which they were not adequately prepared.

Havighurst (1953) carries his analysis beyond the stages of adolescence into adulthood and old age. To the adolescent years he

9

assigns ten tasks, which include achieving mature relations with peers, a masculine or feminine social role, emotional independence from authority, assurance of economic independence, and socially responsible behavior. The other five are accepting and using one's body, selecting and preparing for an occupation, preparing for adult responsibilities, developing skills for civic competence, and acquiring a set of values and an ethical system as a guide to behavior. Young adults between eighteen and thirty are faced with selecting a mate, learning to live with a marriage partner, starting a family, rearing children, managing a home, getting started in an occupation, taking on civic responsibility, and finding a congenial social group. Some would challenge certain of the tasks based on their own individual values, observations, or interpretations of the prevailing culture. Starting a family and rearing children, for instance, may not be viewed as necessary to a particular life style. Nevertheless, people do need to make decisions on these matters even though they choose not to actively participate. That is to say, although not everyone may accomplish a task in the same way, everyone needs to deal with what the task represents in his or her life.

Although he does not call them developmental tasks, Erikson (1963) names five objectives that must be achieved in order to reach the central goal of adolescence—establishing identity. These are learning a masculine or feminine social role, accepting one's body, achieving emotional independence from parents and other adults, selecting and preparing for an occupation, and developing both a scale of values and an ethical system to live by. Note that although Erikson and Havighurst come from different theoretical backgrounds, they generally agree on what youth needs to do in our society.

Somewhat different tasks are outlined by Blocher (1966). For his Exploration Stage (late adolescent–young adult years), Blocher proposed the following: gaining identity as a worker; learning to move from group to individual relationships; achieving emotional autonomy; and producing in work situations. The person must also develop intimacy, commitment, and generativity (the capacity, for example, to commit himself or herself to goals, career, and partner; to be an adequate parent; and give unilaterally). In the Realization Life Stage (thirty to fifty years of age), each individual should learn to be inner directed, become interdependent, handle cognitive dissonance, learn to be flexible and effective emotionally, develop creative thought processes, and establish problem-solving techniques.

Chickering (1969) believes that a new developmental period should be defined in response to the increasing complexity of our time, the fact that 46 percent of the college-age population is enrolled in school because of the increasing demand for skilled and specialized personnel, and the fact that universal higher education is approaching. For this "young adult" stage, he postulates seven major development "vectors."

(1) *Achieving competence.* This involves the development of intellectual and social abilities as well as physical and manual skills. The sense of competence is defined as the confidence individuals have "in their ability to cope with what comes and to achieve successfully what they set out to do."

(2) *Managing emotions.* The young adult's initial task is to become aware of personal feelings and to recognize that they provide information relevant to contemplated behavior or to decisions about future plans. As a larger range of feelings is fully expressed, new and more useful patterns of expression and control can be achieved.

(3) *Becoming autonomous.* Mature autonomy requires both emotional independence—freedom from continual and pressing needs for reassurance and approval—and instrumental independence, the ability to carry on activities and cope with problems without seeking help from others and the ability to be mobile in relation to one's needs. Simultaneously, the individual must accept interdependence, recognizing that one cannot receive benefits from a social structure without contributing to it, that personal rights have a corollary social responsibility.

(4) *Establishing identity.* Identity is confidence in one's ability to maintain inner sameness and continuity; to reach this state, one must understand one's physical needs, characteristics, and personal appearance and be sure of sexual identification and sex-appropriate roles and behavior.

(5) *Freeing interpersonal relationships.* As one matures, one

11

should be able to express greater trust, independence, and individuality in relationships, becoming less anxious and defensive and more friendly, spontaneous, warm, and respectful. Developing tolerance for a wide range of persons is a significant aspect of this task.

(6) *Clarifying purposes.* To develop purpose, an individual must formulate plans and priorities that integrate avocational and leisure-time interests, vocational plans, and life-style considerations.

(7) *Developing integrity.* This task involves making one's values both more personal and more human. One examines and selects "a personally valid set of beliefs that have some internal consistency and provide a guide for behavior." At the same time one drops a literal belief in the absoluteness of rules and adopts a more relative view. Then one must also develop congruence, that is, begin to act in accordance with these personal values.

Still another analyst of this popular subject is Coons (1971), who specifically discusses the tasks of college students. He states that most students move from a child-parent to an adult-adult relationship with their parents, resolve their sexual identity, create a personal value system, develop the capacity for true human intimacy, and choose a life work.

Several developmental tasks of young adults have been specified (Prince, 1973) and published in a *Student Development Task Inventory* (Prince, Miller, and Winston, 1974). They are grouped in nine subtasks under three primary headings. The derivation of most of these categories will be clear. To complete the first task, *developing autonomy,* one must develop emotional and instrumental autonomy, the capacity to live without constant reassurance and approval, independence from parents, and relationships of reciprocal respect with parents and peers alike. One can carry on activities and cope with problems without help from others, be mobile in relation to one's needs and desires, and demonstrate a capacity for self-sufficiency. One is also aware of the relationship between one's behavior and community welfare, develops the ability to contribute to cooperative work, and recognizes that one cannot dispense with one's parents or authorities or accept support without working for it.

Under Task II, *developing mature interpersonal relations,*

one major subtask is developing tolerance. The individual needs to increase his or her capacity to respond to persons in their own right rather than as stereotypes, to develop respect for different backgrounds and values in others, and to resist a need to override others with his or her own ideas. A second subtask, developing mature relationships with peers, requires the person to develop relationships of trust, independence, and individuality, to establish friendships which survive difference and separation, and to respond with warm, open, respectful friendliness as opposed to anxious, defensive, or artificial attitudes. Developing intimate relationships with the opposite sex is a third subtask. To handle this requirement the individual needs to be sensitive to and aware of others' feelings, to develop intimate relationships whose aim is achieving a mutually supportive commitment rather than serving self-discovery, to learn how to love as well as be loved, and to test the ability to make a long-term commitment.

Developing purpose is the third major task; to complete it, the person must develop mature plans for education, career, and life style. Developing educational plans means setting well-defined educational goals, seeing a relationship between study and other aspects of life, becoming aware of the educational setting, and developing good study habits. Career planning includes examining the world of work, understanding the abilities, interests, and values that are needed in various occupations, synthesizing facts and knowledge about oneself and the world of work, and committing oneself to a career and beginning to implement a vocational decision. Finally, a plan for the future that balances vocational aspirations, avocational interests, and family concerns must be developed along with a sense of direction to identify next steps and make a tentative commitment to future plans.

Career Development. The stage and task concepts have been applied to particular kinds of growth, as well as to human development in general. For instance, several theorists and researchers, including Tiedeman and O'Hara (1963), describe vocational tasks. In their career pattern study, Super and his associates (1957, 1963) focused primarily on the "exploratory" and the "establishment" stages of vocational development spanning the years fourteen to

13

twenty-five. The tasks for these periods are to crystallize, specify, and implement a vocational preference, become stable in the chosen vocation, consolidate one's status in that vocation, and then advance in the occupation.

Intellectual Development. Stage theory likewise plays an important role in the work of Piaget (1956), probably the foremost analyst of cognitive development in recent years. He calls the first period the *sensorimotor stage.* Until about age two, the child has no symbolic language, and behavior consists primarily of emotional responses or motor reactions to stimuli. During the *preoperational* stage, from approximately eighteen months to seven years, the child gradually develops the ability to internalize ideas and deal with thoughts about objects rather than directly with the objects themselves. The third stage, according to Piaget, lasts from about age seven until eleven years. In this *concrete operations* stage, the child begins to reason. He or she can serialize and carry out other specific mental operations which, when fully developed, can lead to the final stage of *formal operations.* Now the young person has "adult" thought processes, such as the ability to generate hypotheses and explore them systematically. Thought becomes self-consciously deductive, and the individual learns to organize operations into higher order processes, such as using abstract rules to solve a whole class of problems. Rational, orderly thinking is used to develop problem-solving skills and other abilities. People who have reached the formal operations level tend to be preoccupied with abstraction, and they may develop loyalties not only to people but to ideas. In our culture the ability to perform formal cognitive operations in one's day to day living represents maturity in the eyes of many. And developing these capacities has long been the aim of higher education, often to the neglect of other kinds of development.

Moral Development. According to Kohlberg (1970, 1975), an individual's thinking about moral situations matures through an invariant sequence. In the early years, the child makes moral decisions based totally on avoiding punishment by authorities and then shifts to decisions based on a desire for reciprocity and hedonistic rewards. In the next two stages a desire to please others and receive their approval is the chief motive, followed by a desire to maintain the status quo for its own sake. Two final stages occur during adolescence and young adulthood when decisions result from a recognition of the individual rights of others and social welfare and, ultimately, from an obligation to uphold universal human ethical principles which apply to all mankind. These last two stages, if they occur at all, are likely to begin or be reinforced during the college years and are therefore particularly important to student development educators. In fact, like formal thinking, they may be greatly influenced by higher education.

Other authorities concerned with cognitive, ego, and ethical development who deserve attention include Loevinger (1970), Peck and Havighurst (1960), Kohlberg and Turiel (1971), Galbraith and Jones (1975), McBride (1973), Craig (1974), and Perry (1970).

It seems clear that there is rather strong agreement among human development theorists and researchers on the nature of the developmental needs and derivative tasks which become manifest during the college years. If educational leaders take advantage of this knowledge by giving students opportunities to meet their developmental needs, then students' higher education experiences will be more meaningful and useful to them as productive citizens.

PLANNED CHANGE

After theories come plans. How can desirable development be brought about? We can do our best to design a campus community that nourishes students' growth in all ways. Combs, Avila, and Purkey (1971, p. 220) indicate that change occurs best in atmospheres in which a person feels "that it is safe to try, reassured that he can, encouraged to make the attempts, and satisfied to do so." Other helpful provisions include opportunities for students to reveal their thoughts, feelings, and behavior, seek reactions to what they have revealed, experience a protective atmosphere, seek and receive information, experiment and practice with new ways of thinking and doing, and apply and maintain change within the learning situation (Bradford, 1958). And from the standpoint of behaviorism, Skinner

15

(1974) indicates that a proper learning environment should allow students to move at their own pace, to respond to materials presented and then receive immediate evaluation and reinforcement of their successful responses, and to completely master each step before moving on to the next.

An environment that would provide the foregoing conditions and opportunities can be called a developmental milieu (Blocher, 1966). Its purpose is to plan and bring about change in the institution and all its inhabitants, especially in students, on the assumption that an atmosphere in which change is expected and managed will foster positive development in all. We shall have more to say about creating this milieu later in the book; here we wish to stress the power colleges have to establish this setting and thereby to influence students' lives in an enduring way. As Blocher states, "The college typically has control or could have control over very large parts of the total environment of a population of young people with tremendous capacities for development" (p. 206). And as Feldman and Newcomb (1969, p. 33) conclude:

> One's attitudes and values do not change whimsically, but in response to new information or to new ways of viewing one's world . . . the unique thing about late-adolescence-merging-into-early-maturity is that at this stage of development one is, in our society, maximally motivated to achieve autonomy and at the same time minimally constrained to conform to the restrictions of adult roles. For many of its students, in sum, college-induced changes in attitudes and values are likely to persist. Most of them are not likely again to be so susceptible to new influences, and their college-acquired stances will, to some degree, continue to symbolize independence and adulthood. For some, at least, habits of being open to new information, and being influenced thereby, will result in persisting openness to further change; such an outcome, it may be argued, is one of the goals of a college education.

16

Rationale

Not only do colleges have the power and the opportunity to bring about change, they have the need and the obligation. Some will reject this statement because it seems to have manipulative overtones. Nevertheless, students do seek out higher education for their own betterment. It is higher education's responsibility not to promote regimentation and uniformity, but to offer students an environment in which they learn not just what others have already learned, but also the skills for producing growth in themselves and for creating new knowledge. This is what education and development are all about.

Certain core conditions seem to be essential to creating a truly developmental milieu. In a nonthreatening, supportive environment the individual should: (1) be free to risk disclosure of innermost thoughts and feelings without fear of attack or rejection; (2) be allowed to begin at his or her own level, move at his or her own pace, and master each succeeding level of learning before moving on through the developmental process; (3) have opportunities to identify emerging developmental needs and have an equal voice in deciding what learning to pursue and how to proceed; (4) be able to observe and interact with others who effectively model the characteristics, values, and processes which best represent the outcomes to which the environment is committed; (5) have access to the basic human, physical, monetary, and informational resources necessary for the development being undertaken; (6) receive accurate and usable cognitive and affective feedback and reinforcement in response to behavior; (7) have opportunities to practice and test out new ideas and actions; and (8) be encouraged to learn increasingly complex behavior and apply it, as appropriate, to his or her life situation.

What is required to build this milieu is a thorough knowledge of the campus as an ecological organization, management theory, social systems, and the kinds of student-environment interactions that foster optimum growth. Those who would initiate change must decide on their priorities, plan for contingencies, and make use of the vast body of knowledge available. Certainly, these are tall orders.

17

The Future of Student Affairs

Certainly, creating an atmosphere conducive to deliberate change is an arduous task. Nevertheless we really have no choice but to attempt it. Each of us needs to be the best person we can be, and society depends ultimately on developing that potential.

INTEGRATING PROCESSES

Human beings are integrated wholes. Most of their thinking involves some degree of feeling and body movement. In short, people respond to the world around them as complete organisms and not as components of some larger whole. Although most individuals readily agree with this view, those responsible for social institutions, particularly educators, tend to overlook the implications of this fact in their work. One of the many reasons for higher education's concentration on intellectual development is that the criteria and techniques for measuring noncognitive learning are inadequate. It is extremely difficult to achieve a goal which is unclear and cannot be evaluated. Second, there are quite a few who hold that even if we were able to successfully delineate people's values, beliefs, and emotions, an effort to educate them in these areas is not desirable or appropriate for higher education. Although there has been some movement to overcome such obstacles in recent years (Krathwohl, Bloom and Masia, 1964; Harrow, 1972), those responsible for educational programming have only begun to alter their specific educational goals and curriculum accordingly.

Further, educators have tended to believe that if students develop intellectually they will automatically grow in other ways and therefore educators need not concern themselves with "personal" learning. This rationale, however, has not been supported by the research. Nearly twenty years ago, Jacob (1957) found little evidence, in examining considerable research data, that exposure to a formal academic experience resulted in a significant change in a student's values, beliefs, or personality. More recently, Feldman and Newcomb (1969) noted that although students do seem to be more open to the many facets of the contemporary world and to seek a wider range of contact and experiences as a result of going to college,

18

attendance at college, or the accomplishment of a college degree alone, has few significant effects on students' personal development. These researchers, in fact, contend that perhaps the most notable impact is more a result of accentuating the characteristics which students have when they arrive than a result of the college experience itself. It's very possible that many of our educational approaches engender no more meaningful change than could be expected by chance in any living environment, educationally oriented or not. Further support is provided by a recent study sponsored by the National Institute of Education and carried out by the American Institutes for Research (Wise, 1976). In this eleven-year follow-up to Project Talent, graduates were asked how they feel about their lives now that they are in their thirties. The graduates said they are least satisfied with their intellectual development and with their effort to develop a mature personal understanding of life, two goals with which higher education has supposedly been concerned. Where have we gone wrong?

Clark Kerr recounts how shocked he was when he first heard Aldous Huxley's statement that higher education was going to have to reduce some of its emphasis on the minds of its students and become more concerned with educating their senses. He was, then, probably not as surprised at the results of the Carnegie Commission Study of Academic Opinion: 56,000 of the 70,000 responding undergraduates indicated that colleges must pay more attention to the emotional growth of students and not limit attention to the intellectual (Kerr, 1972). So we have erred in assuming that personal development will take care of itself. But we are beginning to mend our ways. Terms like humanistic education, psychological education, human relations training, and intentional student development have recently emerged in the literature (Mosher and Sprinthal, 1971; Crookston, 1974) along with the beginnings of some systematic programs. More often than not, academic traditionalists look askance at these approaches, but many students are responding positively. And quite a few of these "personal" learning experiences are being offered for credit, a sign that some institutions are coming of age in a full developmental sense.

19

The Future of Student Affairs

The opposites of chance are purpose and intention. What we are proposing, then, is a plan for promoting the kinds of developmental learning and skills that students have identified as desirable for their own life purposes. The principle of intentionality applies not only to program development but to the ability of individuals to identify, create, and use various means for achieving their own goals (Ivey, 1969; Ivey and Rollins, 1972; Ivey and Alschuler, 1973). People who behave intentionally guide their own lives completely and function as self-directing and self-determining human beings. They are not limited to one approach to resolving life problems, nor are they bound by a single course of action. They have the capacity to overcome obstacles and to employ all their human resources to gain their ends. Intentional behavior can be taught and learned in college if the institution is willing to integrate opportunities for physical, emotional, ethical, esthetic, and spiritual development.

The proposed student developmental approach lies somewhere between two opposing theories of education (Havighurst, 1953), that is, somewhere between the theory of freedom, which postulates that the individual develops best when he or she is as unrestricted as possible, and the theory of constraint, which holds that the individual learns to become a worthy, responsible adult by being directed by society. Neither laissez-faire passivity nor authoritarian control is favored. Rather, some middle ground where all members of the academic community have a stake in developing worthy programs and in promoting self-directing, responsible behavior is preferred. Collaboration is preferred to authoritarianism, and prevention and action are more useful than remediation and reaction. Status and position are less important than competence. And confrontation and encountering are better than either control or passivity. Although many colleges give lip service to individual differences and individual development, few comprehensive programs have been designed to help everyone. There are honors programs for the exceptionally gifted, and remedial programs for the exceptionally ungifted or

20

Rationale

academically incompetent, but for the great "silent" majority in the middle, nothing special at all. And for the most part changes occur only when students complain boisterously or when strong pressures are brought to bear.

To counteract these conditions, the intentional student development approach seeks to meet the needs of all students, to plan change rather than react to it, and to engage the full academic community in this collaborative effort. This approach is appropriate not only for young adults but for younger adolescents attending college and older persons who are continuing their education. An eighteen-year-old may be seeking identity or deciding on a career while a sixty-year-old may be contemplating retirement or death. The intentional student development plan can accommodate them because its intent is to meet individuals where they are, developmentally, and help them move on from there. To accomplish these goals, the model has six basic components: goal setting, assessment, instruction, consultation, milieu management, and evaluation. Since each of these is the subject of a chapter, they will be discussed only briefly here—just enough to give a sense of the integrated whole.

An old adage notes, "if you don't know where you're going, you'll never know when you've arrived." Setting goals and establishing specific outcome objectives represent the "mapping" necessary for purposeful development. The educator works with students to determine what they need and want to achieve. When students learn through experience how to set goals, instead of leaving it to others, they have made a good start in planning their growth. Assessment provides the information they need to achieve their aims: it tells them what they know and can do now and what is yet to be accomplished. Like goal setting, assessment is done with students rather than for or about them. It is continuous, it is available to all, and its basic purpose is to help students develop self-evaluation skills that they can use both now and in the future.

The next three components can be seen as strategies for bringing about the desired growth. Instruction, certainly the most familiar and accepted of the three, includes both formal classroom

21

teaching and informal methods for satisfying developmental needs that are not otherwise being met on campus. Any human development task which lends itself to a teaching approach is considered appropriate for inclusion. The consultation strategy assumes that the primary means to self-direction is accepting responsibility for one's development. So the consultant's role is primarily to guide program direction and facilitate action while the client, whether student or colleague, controls the decisions and takes the consequences. Consultation is particularly valuable for establishing growth-producing colleague relationships.

Milieu management is probably the most complex and least understood strategy. The term *milieu* refers to the physical environment, the human community, the curriculum, and other aspects of the students' world. The term *management,* however, is not synonymous with control. Rather, it means a collaborative effort to coordinate resources and design activities that will establish a developmental climate for growth.

The competence of the student development educator will be especially tested by planning the best strategies and carrying them out. He or she must have accurate information on people's needs, know how to meet them, and be skilled at responding to the uniqueness of a given individual, group, or organization. The educator should be familiar with the available resources and opportunities and be able to create new ones when necessary. Devising a feasible, concrete strategy that the student can implement is essential as is the institution's ability to help the student carry out this plan.

The nature of the final component, evaluation, is probably evident. Here, it refers to student development programs and their staff members, not to students, whose success is measured as part of the assessment process. The evaluator should first examine how well the goals and objectives of the planned programs relate to those of the participants and then how well these aims are being achieved. If accountability and long-term success are to be had, evaluation is essential, for it not only shows what has happened so far but provides a sound basis for modification and future planning. However, it must be an integral part of the program from the beginning.

Rationale

DOMAINS OF STUDENT DEVELOPMENT

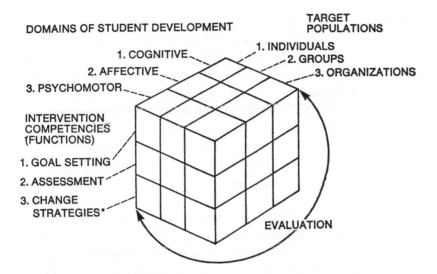

*INSTRUCTION, CONSULTATION, and MILIEU MANAGEMENT

FIGURE 1. Student Development Model

Figure 1 represents an attempt to graphically depict the student development model. The cube form expresses the interrelatedness of all the components. The fourth dimension, evaluation, encompasses the whole cube, symbolizing the importance of comprehensive program evaluation to the student development model.

OPERATIONAL CHALLENGES

Basically, the purpose for creating the intentional student development plan is to offer postsecondary institutions an alternative to test out and apply in the years ahead. The challenges of adopting such an approach are many. First, the way we view students and how they spend their time in colleges must change. We must stop looking at them "as passive vessels eternally ready to contain any content we provide" (Ivey and Alschuler, 1973, p. 593) and see them more in terms of their own developmental needs. This perceptual change calls for an accompanying shift in our professional role as we focus less on programs and more on learners who are growing. If the principle that human development is cumulative and continuous is adopted, then our primary task is helping students acquire the skills and knowledge they need in order to change. If the concept that individuals should master certain developmental tasks in a given life stage is adopted, our role is to help students understand those tasks and complete them at the appropriate time.

The comprehensive student development approach calls for the development and participation of the whole academic community. Dissolution of the invisible but too often impregnable walls between various groups and departments on campus is essential, as is not becoming bogged down with the irrelevant tasks and pressures often found in a bureaucracy. Problems and crises must be handled, yet the greater challenge is to shape the campus environment creatively so that its inhabitants can change in positive ways. Although the magnitude of this challenge is great, it can be met by active, organized, and committed student development educators.

Among the other challenges to the student affairs staff and faculty are the following:

• To contribute to our knowledge of students in higher education by defining the types of growth that take place and the order in which they occur.

• To develop strategies for getting the goal of student development adopted as a primary aim of higher education.

• To find ways to contribute to the development of the total population on campus, not just to the remediation of a few.

• To develop collaborative programming with other student affairs departments and with academic departments.

• To identify, stimulate, and reward the participation of faculty members in nonacademic areas of college life.

• To understand human development and the student development model and fit that model to one's immediate situation.

• To provide the data and build the kinds of relationships that will motivate individuals, groups, and organizations to take responsibility for setting goals.

• To develop techniques for teaching self-assessment skills to individuals, groups, and organizations.

24

Rationale

- To plan and present courses that promote both affective and cognitive development so that they will be incorporated in the curriculum.
- To introduce developmental goals into existing college courses.
- To develop ways of overcoming the forces that prevent student development educators from consulting effectively with the faculty or administration.
- To balance the ethical concerns that arise from trying to change people indirectly by altering the environment with the need to see that environmental characteristics support the development of human beings.
- To answer the question "To whom are we accountable?"
- To move from traditional models of student personnel work to the student development model without undue stress and anxiety.
- To find ways of communicating our new roles and the purposes of our new functions as student development educators to the rest of the campus—students, faculty members, and administrators.

Higher education in the future needs to respond both to students and to the needs of the larger community within which it functions. Holding to the elitism and essentialism which once stood higher education in good stead is not useful today, let alone tomorrow. Institutions of higher learning will flounder if they persist in sequestered and archaic approaches to instruction and control by a limited few. Instead, they must face the future squarely with resolution and the knowledge that all things do change with time and the survivors are those that anticipate, respond to, and flow with that change. Let higher education not only be a survivor, but a leader. It can be if it will clarify its aims and then rise to the challenge of achieving them. Although no magic formulas are offered, the intentional student development model presented in this book can help many academic communities shape the future rather than merely adjust to it.

25

Chapter 2

❧❧❧❧❧❧❧❧

Setting Goals

Developmental change in students does not occur automatically and may not even take a positive direction. Because growth is a continuous, though not necessarily uniform, process, it is important to guide it by establishing some aims and directions. This goal setting should be a collaborative effort by students or other groups and student development educators to determine the specific values, abilities, states of being, or general levels of proficiency which those persons want to attain.

Although the terms *goal* and *objective* are often used interchangeably, for our purposes they are defined differently. A goal is a general, somewhat long-range target or aim; an objective, on the other hand, is a precise statement that establishes specific expectations, states how much time should be required to meet those expectations, and sets a standard of excellence which can be easily evaluated (Stimpson and Simon, 1974). Thus, goal setting is the process of stating the general outcome desired and then defining the more specific results (objectives) that guide the steps in achieving the goals and that provide evidence of accomplishment.

Since the general goal of student development is healthy functioning, the objectives that support this aim identify those skills or tasks which need to be mastered to effect self-direction and self-determination. The purpose of the goal-setting process is to offer individuals a means to find out where they want to go and how they want to get there. This method gives them an opportunity to anticipate future problems and needs and to take action before a crisis is reached. By promoting positive change, setting goals also tends to inhibit the development of personal or group problems. Finally, determining aims is an important part of the student development model simply because little of consequence has ever been achieved by humanity without a goal.

INDIVIDUAL GOALS AND PROGRAM GOALS

Although this chapter focuses primarily on setting goals for individuals rather than for developmental programs, many procedures are the same for both. In the past, program staff members have stressed activities more than students' learning, but in the student development model, program goals are the outcomes expected from students' participation in a given developmental activity. Stating objectives in this way directs attention to the student and to the types of behavior he or she is expected to exhibit as a result of a particular experience. This shift in focus—from the student affairs staff to the student and from the activity to the result— should be the intent of developmental programming and should establish a framework for selecting evaluation criteria and procedures. In effect, the student developmental model emphasizes students as developing learners instead of the programs developed to serve them.

27

In clarifying the important distinction between activity goals and developmental outcomes, the following examples may be useful. An activity-oriented objective might be "To give students the tools of leadership and management." An outcome objective, on the other hand, might be "The student can distinguish between authoritarian and democratic styles of leadership by identifying five or more specific differences exhibited by the two types of leaders." The second objective specifies the behavior a student will demonstrate as a result of attending a workshop on leadership training. The words "to give students," in the first statement, emphatically imply that the student affairs professional, not the student, is engaging in an activity. The focus clearly is on what will be done rather than on what the student will learn.

A broader example of the student-centered approach is the Individual Development: Encounter with the Arts and Sciences (IDEAS) program at Austin College in Sherman, Texas. Here, the growth of each individual student is paramount; no monolithic system has been formulated for some imaginary "average" student and imposed on all. In this program the traditional roles of teacher and student are changing. As the professor becomes a "facilitator" instead of an authority, the student must assume the major responsibility for his or her own learning. The traditional task of merely providing the student with factual knowledge is evolving into one of working with each student and his or her personal interests, needs, and goals. IDEAS at Austin College represents changes throughout all parts of the curriculum.

Central to IDEAS is the program called Individual Development (I.D.), a comprehensive but personal advising system in which each student has a faculty mentor and through which the concerns of the student, often found outside the classroom, move into the mainstream of the educational program. In I.D. the student and the mentor together plan a program fitted to the student's individual needs and goals. Individual Development is a *process* based on the rationale that each student should be actively involved in planning all aspects of his or her education and in working toward unity, integrity, and meaningfulness. Sometimes putting these plans into writing or just discussing them verbally, the student and mentor decide on action to be taken in the areas of academic, societal/social, religious/philosophical, aesthetic, vocational, and physical development.

What emerges in Individual Development might look something like this:

Physical Profile. Goals: Develop a healthy level of physical fitness; learn a variety of sports and physical activities that will enable you to remain fit throughout life. Means: Complete the physical profile; take physical activity courses; carry out a program of physical activity on your own; engage in intramural sports; swim or work out in the exercise room regularly; jog or take a walk or bicycle.

Societal/Social Profile. Goals: Gain the knowledge and experience that will help you be a responsible citizen and a participating member of society; become better informed about social issues; become involved in civic activities. Means: Read newspapers and current periodicals; attend pertinent lectures and films; watch TV news and documentary programs; take courses in social science, history, and other pertinent fields; work in campus government and organizations or programs like voter registration, Boys' Club, and civic orchestra; vote.

An important factor in the developmental process for the advisee, as well as the mentor, is evaluation of the assessment process. Each academic year, the professor is asked to complete a report on each advisee's progress. The student may meet with the faculty member to discuss involvement in each of the various development areas, or the student may be asked to write a summary of activities and then arrange for a conference. The mentor will evaluate whether the student has satisfactorily demonstrated responsible action in achieving set goals. If, in the student's opinion, the mentor's evaluation is incorrect or the mentor has incompletely understood the degree of actual involvement, the advisee may write a rebuttal in which he or she cites items of individual development omitted or misinterpreted by the mentor. Each evaluation must be a questioning, continuing analysis of the student's participation, rather than merely a final report.

29

The I.D. course begins, then, when the mentor and student jointly assess the student's current level of achievement—and not just in intellectual skills, but vocational, aesthetic, religious, social, and physical development, too. With this assessment, they plan the steps needed to reach his or her personal goals and the standards of the college. Assessment and planning, including the preparation and regular updating of a total educational plan, continue throughout the college years, and at the end of the senior year, the student receives one course credit for successfully completing the I.D. program.

The learning experiences provided by any student development program are not ends in themselves but means to ends. The process of development (programming) and the products (behavioral outcomes) must not be confused. Stating objectives in terms of the learning process is misleading, because one experience may contribute to many different kinds of learning and a particular outcome may be derived from many different learning experiences.

Stating program goals as the results of learning contributes to development in the following ways:

(1) It provides direction for student affairs professionals and clearly conveys their intent to others.

(2) It guides the selecting of experiences to be offered by the program.

(3) It establishes a framework for evaluating student achievement.

(4) If the proposed learning outcomes are clear to the student, they help to direct both the formal and informal learning activities.

Program goals are established by the student affairs worker in collaboration with the student, usually at the program's inception. The fact that a student participates in a given activity in no way guarantees that the preestablished goals and objectives are owned by that individual. A major problem in the field has been that even well-planned, well-implemented programs failed because their goals were not congruent with those of the individual participants. If students first determine their aims and if student affairs workers respond by establishing appropriate objectives for the programs they develop, then the chance of matching an individual with a helpful program is increased immeasurably.

Since setting goals establishes guidelines for planned growth, it helps ensure that all changes are positive steps toward achievement. Students develop a sense of worth and power when they discover their ability to influence their own development. It's often exciting to watch them learn what they can do to attain their objectives and then organize their efforts into useful activities. When students determine their own goals, they are far more likely to learn to take responsibility for their own learning, because worthwhile, attainable goals are excellent motivators. Similarly, students can measure their own performance because they already have goals to serve as criteria. Like all of us, they definitely gain a better self-concept when they see clear evidence that they really are growing.

Students aren't the only ones who benefit. Having objectives helps the student affairs staff to select growth-producing activities and to individualize their programming by producing the particular experiences a student requires. Student affairs workers are forced to take a look at their practices to be sure they are supporting the aims of individual students.

When students decide where they are going, the staff members have a way not only to assess the student's progress, but to judge their own effectiveness as well. This capacity is increasingly important, because as demands for accountability grow, the process of choosing aims and writing objectives by students and staff alike will help to establish the necessary evaluation programs. True, goal setting is not an end in itself, but it does establish both the starting line and the destination.

The ultimate benefit of this whole procedure is that as individuals and groups learn to formulate their own behavioral objectives, they will carry their skills into the larger community and into the rest of their lives. So it is essential that students be taught *how* to choose rather than *what* to choose.

As stated, systematic development does not just happen; it must be purposely triggered and carefully nurtured if the individual's full potential is to be fulfilled (Blocher, 1974), and goal setting

31

often acts as this trigger. The kinds of goals that are appropriate for each person are suggested by the developmental stage theory outlined earlier. Developmental tasks, like other, more formal subjects, can be systematized. Just as there is a certain content to be mastered in history or chemistry, there are certain types of knowledge or skills that must be attained if an individual is to progress to the next life stage. Goal setting can help accomplish each of these tasks as they appear. The developmental task theory also allows the student affairs worker to specify much more concretely the objectives of any intervention and to classify activities that support or reinforce developmental task mastery.

SOURCES OF GOALS AND OBJECTIVES

Since the needs of the individual energize his or her actions, the behavioral changes needed or desired by each individual constitute the foundation for developmental goals. But these expectations clearly do not exist in a vacuum. They are shaped by the value structures of the culture, so a student's goal statements must be meaningful in his or her own life situation. Goals that are created cooperatively by the student and the educator are particularly valuable because they combine the student's felt needs and the educator's personal theory of development and knowledge of the process involved. A one-sided determination is likely to have shortcomings.

What kinds of goals are these collaborators apt to choose? The developmental literature is full of terms like self-fulfillment, self-actualization, and self-direction. But these ultimates are helpful only in general ways, for they seem to have little direct connection with most student affairs programs. Obviously, abstract aims alone are not enough to activate developmental programs. What does make a difference, however, is the educator's knowledge of developmental tasks and his or her skill at helping the students formulate specific objectives. These tasks provide relatively discrete reference points on which the student development educator and the student can focus attention.

32

Setting Goals

Zaccaria (1965) proposed a hierarchial structure in which completing an adequate set of subdevelopmental tasks (and thereby achieving short-term goals) helps the individual undertake basic developmental tasks and reach intermediate goals. Mastery of these basic tasks brings happiness and satisfaction as well as leads toward achievement of the broader aims like self-fulfillment, self-direction, and self-actualization.

In setting up this hierarchy, the student affairs worker must try to help the student establish a balance between personal uniqueness and commonalities with others. Generally speaking, developmental tasks are required of all individuals in a given culture, yet each task has a unique meaning to each person and will be mastered in accordance with special characteristics, such as age, sex, and temperament (Zaccaria, 1965).

Another source of goals is the value system of the student affairs worker. At some point, the desirability of certain aims must be evaluated, and since values are implicit in every action taken, the professional cannot and should not try to eliminate them from the goal-setting process. Part of the educator's role is to help individuals use their intellects and emotions to analyze their situation, identify and evaluate alternative value systems, and examine the conse-quences of different answers to moral and ethical questions. When it is appropriate, educators need not hesitate to make clear their own positions so long as they avoid imposing their values and do not attempt to persuade students to imitate them.

STATING GOALS AND OBJECTIVES

Goal setting requires active participation by both the student and the student development educator. Four specific steps guide the process of shaping goals into achievable entities.

(1) *Identify the overall goal and state it in written form.* State the general outcome(s) expected from completing a developmental task or subtask. Putting the goal in writing helps everyone delineate what he or she is trying to do and gives the educator and the student a tangible objective with which to work. Ambiguous

33

verbal statements are usually profitless and may easily lead to conflicts.

(2) *Identify and list the specific behaviors which would satisfy both the student and the educator that the goal has been achieved.* This is a process of refining and getting down to the "nitty-gritty"—the immediate objectives and the observable performance that will prove their attainment. The particular behaviors identified are only a sample of the learning outcomes which could be included. The list might be lengthened, shortened, or modified according to the developmental needs of the student. The sorting and weighing of possibilities should result in a set of discrete results on which both the student and the educator can agree.

(3) *Write a statement for each behavior which clearly describes the nature, quality, or quantity of a minimum performance.* In this important step the collaborators try to express as clearly as they can the discrete actions which, as a whole, represent the behavior of an individual who has accomplished a given goal. The specific procedures recommended for defining behavioral objectives include the following.

A. State each objective using an active verb that denotes observable behavior, for instance, "Demonstrate the ability . . . , decide upon . . . , write a statement . . . "

B. State objectives in terms of student performance rather than in terms of student affairs program performance. "Join two campus organizations . . . , complete an assertiveness training workshop."

C. State objectives as learning outcomes rather than as processes. For example, "Write a ten-sentence paragraph without grammatical errors . . . , verbally communicate disagreement with another's position."

D. Indicate the expected terminal behavior instead of stating only the content of the desired change: "Pass an interpersonal relations competence test at an 80 percent level of accuracy . . . , obtain a date with a member of the opposite sex."

E. Include only one learning outcome, not a combination of several outcomes. "Change a car's tire" or "Change a car's oil," rather than "Perform general maintenance on a car."

F. Make each objective specific enough to clearly indicate both the desired results and the expected student behavior. "Exhibit leadership ability by heading a committee in club X and complete assigned task by the established deadline date."

In addition, the student and the educator should agree beforehand on the circumstances of how, where, and when mastery of the objective will be demonstrated. Establishing the level of acceptable achievement tells the student how well he or she must perform for the objective to be accomplished.

It's probably obvious that cognitive and physical goals lend themselves to behavioral objectives. Affective aims, on the other hand, which are concerned with feelings and attitudes, are usually achieved internally. This problem is not insurmountable, however, for affective behavior can often be stated in terms of external and observable activity also. To write an affective objective, then, the student and educator must identify some observable activity which both accept as evidence that the desired internal changes have occurred. For example, to demonstrate tolerance the student might exhibit open-minded behavior such as listening closely to others' points of view, not making rash or uncomplimentary statements about others, and so on.

(4) *Evaluate the performance statements by determining whether the student and the educator agree that the goal will have been achieved when the student exhibits the behaviors as stated.* This final reexamination should answer questions like, Have we left anything essential out? Or have we included some nonessentials? As part of this evaluation, the collaborators might review the following definitions. A *long-range goal* requires an extended period of time to accomplish, perhaps as much as several years. A *short-range goal* can be accomplished in a relatively short time, perhaps a day or week or month or college term. A *behavioral goal* is behavior that is observable or measurable. A *nonbehavioral goal* is more abstract in concept and involves attitudes, traits of character, or other personal characteristics that cannot be easily measured or observed. A *realistic goal* can be attained, whereas an unrealistic goal cannot be achieved by anyone with similar ability under similar circumstances. A *meaningful goal* can be reached because it is clearly defined, but a mean-

ingless goal is too broad to be pursued and too irrelevant for the student to value as worth pursuing.

Since goal setting for student development has a special purpose, the student and the educator might also ask themselves the following related questions as a way of appraising their work. Has the student said that the objectives are appropriate, valuable, and relevant? Are the objectives logical developmental outcomes? Can the objectives be attained by the student(s) involved? Are the objectives in harmony with the dominant cultural norms of the individual and the institution? Are they also in harmony with the basic principles of human development? Are the objectives integrated within the total development process so that their outcomes can be transferred to continued advanced-level development?

Probably a counseling or advising relationship is the best context for learning how to set goals, although the basic skills may be gained in other milieus. For instance, the goal-setting process is an integral part of a decision-making training program developed by the College Entrance Examination Board (Gelatt and others, 1973). Likewise, Management by Objectives (MBO) programs include goal setting as a tool for facilitating organizational development. As individuals learn to formulate group and organizational goals, the more effective functioning that results is likely to improve the quality of their individual lives as well.

Another example of this training is a comprehensive program called "Risking Change: Goal Setting for Personal and Professional Development." In the one-day mini-workshop, offered by the State University College at Buffalo, participants use a set of goal-setting skills to develop an action program for their own personal and professional growth. The primary objectives are (1) to develop the ability to anticipate and embrace the risks and rewards involved in goal setting and (2) to design and then implement the concrete change activities needed to accomplish these goals.

The workshop is designed to encourage each group member to become explicitly conscious of his or her strengths, likes, and evolving interests. This inventory of "what I am good at," "what I like," and "what I want to be" can relate to a number of developmental needs: improving relations with friends, or family, or colleagues; setting personal objectives concerned with anything from exploration of certain aspects of the personality to the development of certain abilities or interests; and making professional or career choices. Each participant is then encouraged to establish his or her own priorities and to translate those "I want" goal statements into concrete action programs. An assessment of present strengths and abilities, rather than a list of all the resources needed to attain these goals, gives each person a "reality map" of potential change activities. This map acts as a guide to embracing those specific actions that are essential in effectively determining one's own future.

The exercises and interactions, which include individual worksheet exercises, small group interactions, short lectures on the techniques of planned change, and experiences in trying out "risk" and "change" behavior, are deliberately designed to be flexible and to evoke open exploration. Thus they must remain pliable, responsive to any variation on the main theme. The dynamic relation between the participants and their materials naturally produces suggestions on how an exercise can best be used or modified, how the flow of interaction can be recontoured to reflect immediate needs, and how other exercises or dynamics can be used—in the next hour, or next session, or next workshop.

Various means are used to evaluate the materials and the progress of the participants as the workshop moves along. The leader monitors the verbal and body language of the participants to be sure that instructions and exercises are clearly presented, to find out who needs personal attention and who needs more or less time to work through an exercise or an interaction. Checks on the clarity of materials and progress in—or anxiety about—risking change are also obtained periodically as by-products of sharing observations in trios and quartets. The leader is always available to answer questions, to respond to individual needs, and to encourage or "grant permission" for exploring self and risking change.

The workshop is scheduled so that the leader has time to interact with each participant while other individuals or small groups continue to work on an exercise. And since the leader also takes the workshop, he or she is constantly part of the group, is a member of the break-out trios and quartets, and experiences first-hand the process of exploring and responding to the materials and exercises. This direct involvement is an excellent way of assessing the clarity and effectiveness of materials and of gaining a real understanding of the experiences and observations of the "other" participants.

The following are some specific objectives that have been established and sometimes achieved during the workshop:

(1) Discover my interests, abilities, and achievements.

(2) Monitor my use of time and identify the motivations behind my activities; separate "I want" from "I should."

(3) Identify my images of my potential and clarify my goals.

(4) Plan and implement an action program which involves the risk of change: reorganize my activities to support my images of my potential and help me attain my future goals—that is, maximize "I want" activities and diminish the activities guided by motivations of "I should" and "I always have."

(5) Develop confidence in risk-taking and in change behavior.

(6) Complete a life plan by formulating specific goals, objectives, timetables, and evaluation techniques.

(7) Initiate and celebrate the rewards of change and risk.

One of the unique characteristics of the workshop is that it is open to persons of all ages (almost—they must be over twelve) and educational backgrounds. It can be offered to undergraduate or graduate students as a group. It can be used by a group of professional staff members for their own individual development. Or enrollment can be more open-ended and heterogeneous if the workshop is offered in the evening, on a weekend, or as part of a program of lifelong learning for all interested parties. This last approach is especially attractive to the designer of the workshop, because the participants can encounter change and risk as human problems independent of status, or profession, or age.

Thus, some persons use the workshop to plan for retirement; others are conscious of choosing a mate; others want to explore new careers; still others use the process to choose a major in college, select

38

a life style, explore an interest or hobby, or simply broaden their horizons and concept of self. The process is the same for all persons, but the specific outcomes are quite different.

The workshop emphatically asserts that change and risk are integral to the goal-setting process, which entails hard work, honesty, openness to change, and concrete action programs. These realities are not avoided; they are joined, tackled, and celebrated in an atmosphere of permission and support from the leader and, slowly but surely, from the entire group.

The entire workshop—all of its exercises, materials, interactions—is designed to help the group members (a) make their needs and interests and skills and goals *conscious and emphatic;* (b) translate those conscious feelings and thoughts into *written form* for study, retrieval, and recurring integration; and (c) activate those feelings and thoughts in concrete (written) *action programs.*

Another workshop that incorporates goal setting is the Program for the Development and Training of Student Leaders at Wesleyan College, Macon, Georgia. Its purpose is to improve the quality of management of campus activities and organizations. The program consists of a concentrated two-day conference and an ongoing inservice program conducted throughout the year. Faculty advisors of the specific organizations attend all the sessions and meet as a group during the two-day conference. During that meeting, they formulate their goals as advisors and propose methods of evaluating the student leaders.

The general goals of the workshop are to increase student leaders' awareness of how to administer/manage organizations and to give them the appropriate tools to achieve these aims. The participants formulate measurable objectives for their organizations and develop a handbook/calendar that could be used throughout the year and passed on to future leaders.

Three strategy and model-building sessions occur. During the first one, students are asked to do the following as a group: Define the mission or purpose of your club/organization and publication; write a minimum of five goals for the year for your club/organization and publication; describe at least two ways of accomplishing each of these five goals; establish a tentative daily, weekly, and monthly timetable; draw up an organization chart by function; assign the functions to an office, if possible; formulate an agenda for your club/organization/publication meetings; list five long-range goals for your club/organization.

In the second session individuals are to: polish up the organization chart by function and job; write a job description for your general office—president, secretary, vice president, and so on; write a minimum of five objectives for your general office, and place them in a time sequence; and list two long-range goals for your specific office. During the third session, individual students are given directions along the same lines: write a more detailed description of your specific job; write a minimum of ten personal objectives for your specific job (can include some of same ones used in other two sessions); prepare a log or diary which includes a timetable showing when you will do these tasks; draw up a checklist to determine how you know the job has been accomplished; and list five personal career goals.

Student leaders evaluate their own progress by examining their stated measurable goals and objectives. An individual conference between the faculty advisor and each student leader is conducted several times during the year.

APPLICATION

The goals have been set by the student or group in cooperation with the student affairs worker, the objectives have been written, and acceptable levels of performance have been agreed upon. Now what? Unfortunately, it is more difficult to describe precisely the steps of implementation than to discuss goal setting, although the latter is probably half the battle, for well-defined aims clarify the means as well as the ends. Once the students have decided which objective has top priority, they should identify what resources are available—both within themselves and in the environment. The educator can be particularly useful at this point by helping the student find and select the most appropriate options. After the student determines how best to use resources, the collaborators work out a strategy, one that will not close off other goals should the first one not be achieved. The plan should permit the resources to be managed in such a way that there will be enough left over to pursue an alternate venture.

For example, a student set as a goal for herself for fall semester of her freshman year "To learn how to express more honestly my needs and desires to my roommate." A step-by-step plan was set up with the aid of an advisor:

(1) Attend an assertiveness training session
    (a) learn what my interpersonal rights are
    (b) learn how to stand up for my rights without infringing on the rights of my roommate
    (c) practice expressing my feelings in an honest way
(2) Select one specific behavior of my roommate and give her feedback about how it bothers me (for instance, when she comes in at night after I have gone to bed and turns on all the lights) and then work with her to solve the problem
(3) Report back to my advisor on my feelings and success or failure with this specific objective
(4) Select a more difficult source of conflict and express my feelings to my roommate about it
(5) Evaluate the quality of my assertive expressions and how I feel after expressing them
(6) If this strategy does not yield success, choose an alternate strategy

Students setting out on this journey need continuing support, additional data, feedback on progress, and probably some old-fashioned "hand-holding," too. The student development educator needs great skill, a quantity of patience, and a sensitive understanding of human dynamics to help students set their goals and then follow through on them. A specific plan for continuing evaluation should be created and agreed to, because regular meetings not only boost the student's will power and redirect faltering steps, but show the educator how the student is doing. In addition, this feedback process stresses their mutual responsibilities and gives them a chance

The Future of Student Affairs

to rework poorly planned objectives. The student will learn the value of and feel the need for applying a systematic goal-setting procedure only when he or she has positive experiences using it. The individual can learn to choose those goals that will truly further development only when opportunities have been provided to clarify personal needs and to act on them. The student affairs professional can encourage this learning process immeasurably by establishing a relationship with the student which demonstrates that the student's developmental needs are a main concern and that helping the student meet those needs is a primary goal.

ROLE OF THE STUDENT DEVELOPMENT EDUCATOR

The job of the student affairs worker is not solely that of assisting individual students. As Shaffer (1973) has stated, the professional can contribute to the total development of colleges and universities by helping to clarify organization goals. Shaffer's research has indicated that more often than not institutional actions are not based on a conscious review of their stated aims. If the institution states that individual development is one of its major concerns, then practices must exemplify that ideal. In most cases, individual development has not been defined specifically enough to make it realizable in practice, so meaningless generalizations about educational goals have tended to float, unattached, above "business as usual." This failure of administrators to translate general goals into operational guidelines may have widened the gulf between students and administration. The student affairs staff can play a significant role in policy making by insisting that fundamental goals and objectives be the basis for action.

Nevertheless, the primary task of these staff members is helping individual and groups of students establish and implement their aims. To this end, the student affairs worker needs some particular skills and abilities. First, he or she should be familiar with various "values clarification" approaches and be able to assist students in identifying what they prize, cherish, and believe. Unless students'

42

interests and aptitudes are clarified, it is difficult to determine whether their objectives are realistic. When values are vague and inconsistent, they generate aimless and confused goals.

Second, the student affairs worker should know what general and specific outcomes can normally be expected from completing the various developmental tasks. Using current knowledge in the field, he or she can help students find out what kinds of behavior are usually correlated with success and happiness in life. Third, as pointed out earlier, the student development educator should be skilled at using the goal-setting process and at teaching others how to apply it. This ability is especially important because the way in which goals and objectives are stated affects the students' future. The fourth needed skill is a subtle one—being able to motivate students and get them to take responsibility for setting goals and making decisions. The steps in learning how to establish objectives are time-consuming and difficult, yet some students expect to achieve their goals without commitment, hard work, or taking risks. Likewise, not all individuals are able to achieve all their aims on the first try and may, as a result, become disillusioned and ready to quit. The educator must be competent at dealing with such individuals in ways that will ultimately promote their growth. Finally, the student affairs staff member needs consultation skills in order to help students locate the settings in which their particular goals and objectives may best be mastered.

He or she should know what institutional and community resources are available and be able to show students how they can use these resources for advancing their present development. One model effort is the Career Action Commission set up at the University of Nebraska at Lincoln, which attempts to help the faculty, students, and staff learn about those with particular expertise in the community who, because of their experiences and training, can assist students with their career concerns. Such individuals and groups include the Chamber of Commerce, the City Council, educational television professionals, labor unions, public school counselors, ministers, and so on. The Commission not only wants to make existing resources scattered throughout the university and the larger community more visible to the public, but also to better coordinate existing services and restructure outmoded programs.

There are a number of publications that can help working professionals improve their abilities. Although many of them are concerned with instructional goals, they can be valuable to the student affairs worker. Excellent resources include Plowman (1971), Gronlund (1970), and Mager (1962, 1972). Useful information about the characteristics of goals and objectives is found in three books on their taxonomic structures (Bloom, 1956; Krathwohl and others, 1964; Harrow, 1972). Because this system assumes that the results of learning can best be described in terms of changes in student behavior, it is a useful guide to educators who wish to state their program objectives in behavioral terms. Still another source of relevant material is the literature on management by objectives, a currently popular approach. Although these publications tend to focus on administration, the skills needed for establishing goals and objectives are the same. Some pertinent references include Drucker (1954), Odiorne (1965), Likert (1967), Harvey (1972), McAshan (1974), Heaton (1975), and Deegan and Fritz (1975).

PROBLEMS AND CONCLUSIONS

The difficulties inherent in setting goals should be identified so that student development educators can take steps to overcome them in planning their programs. No doubt most of you are aware of the quantification problems, for instance. Measuring growth and development is a complex task because its manifestations, especially the emotional ones, are somewhat abstract, and objectives are very difficult to state in measurable terms. And the whole theoretical and conceptual aspect of student development needs additional attention. Cross (1973) suggests that we just don't know enough about student development to begin to train applied behavioral scientists to bring it about. Further research is needed to extend and refine our knowledge of these complex processes. However, the model presented in this book offers an excellent opportunity for testing out some of the basic knowledge currently available about human development.

Another familiar problem is money. Budget limitations often block the use of an individualized program for student development, yet student affairs programs can begin to move by improving the group learning experiences offered in colleges and universities and focusing on developmental processes throughout the institution, including the academic curriculum. Although an individual approach is sometimes desirable, the many developmental commonalities among college students allow group work to be effective and useful, as was shown in our earlier description of the Buffalo workshop.

Finally, some persons feel there is an inherent contradiction between an objectified goal-setting process and the aim of developing a self-actualizing and fully functioning person. In response to this criticism, Cohen and Hersh (1972) have postulated that "behavorial humanism" can integrate the two orientations by combining the strengths of the humanists—providing direction and rationales for goals—with those of the behaviorists—establishing attainable and measurable goals and having techniques to effect and systematically evaluate the desired results. Such an eclectic approach, which is a foundation of this student developmental model, will be useful in facilitating human development.

Chapter 3

Assessing Individual Growth

Although assessment is basic to full development, most current definitions limit its potential contribution. As some see it, assessment is the establishment of a collegewide testing program directed by a specialist in testing and statistical analysis, but this view is narrow and mechanistic. Others interpret assessment as evaluation, a terminal step which gives little or no attention to the value judgments involved. For still others, assessment means using special techniques to better understand a given individual, group, or organization—a worthy-sounding goal—yet they assign full responsibility to the professional staff instead of to the student or group. In this situation, the student affairs worker is an authority who directs students' behavior. As a direct result of these and similar conceptions, students have too often been seen as objects to be assigned to categories or classifications or described in terms that are meaningful only to the evaluator. Student affairs workers who limit their view of assessment to the measurement of traits, abilities, and similar variables often pay little attention to the environment that affects those variables. So although assessment is considered important by many, it may not promote the development of students if it is viewed too narrowly. To increase its contribution, this function must be broadened and placed in a more central role by student development educators.

Brown (1972), Grant (1972), and Parker (1973), among others, have suggested some future directions. Referring to those who accomplish the assessment task as diagnosticians, Brown indicates that they rarely examine the student's total developmental history and potential. For many students, assessment occurs only when they are first being admitted to college or when they are trying to choose an academic major. Often these efforts stress academic abilities or career aptitudes and omit such important characteristics as social skills and receptivity to new ideas. Grant points out that when students first enter college, they should be interviewed immediately so that the present status of their development will be known to those who want to help them further their growth. This assessment would serve as the basis for determining the goals they wish to achieve throughout the college years. Parker calls for assessment procedures that can be used by the faculty, instead of by professional psychologists alone, and that measure progress toward well-defined educational objectives.

Assessment for student development, then, is the process through which *students, groups,* and *organizations* systematically acquire and use data from a variety of sources to describe, appraise, and modify *their own development.* Thus, this method differs from the more traditional approaches in its purpose, in what is assessed, in the techniques used, in the way it is implemented, and in the role the student affairs practitioner plays.

This active, positive stand can be contrasted with the remedial focus of many existing programs. Too often their primary objective has been to classify students using supposedly valid standardized tests. The effect on students who have been labeled inferior has often been negative. If assessment focuses on identifying those behaviors which students failed to attain or master according to a preestablished normative standard, then remedial programs will usually be designed to develop them. As a consequence, when assessment data show that a student is functioning "normally," no one tries very hard to encourage the development of additional desirable behaviors. These remedial approaches have been justified in part because they produce a manageable population with which to work and in part because the students involved seem more likely to fail in society than do the "normally functioning" students. The question is, however, Can we afford to retain such narrow goals and still meet the needs of students now and in the future?

Assessment for student development, unlike remediation, is a broad function and a vital part of the total growth process. Its object is to help students understand their current patterns of behavior, emphasizing positively the specific skills they have instead of the ones they lack. From this base, *all* students can move toward increased self-direction.

Many existing assessment programs have made little attempt to help students find out how well they are growing outside the cognitive domain. Although most postsecondary institutions have a published commitment to educating the "total student," they have given little real attention to specifying and encouraging positive interests, attitudes, values, and appreciations. The failure of students to examine such personal growth dimensions as they progress through formal education programs could lead to their neglect and to an overemphasis on purely intellectual attainments. Instead of being a peripheral function, assessment of emotional, social, aesthetic, cultural, and even physical development should be as systematically organized as the evaluation of cognition has been. Moreover, this kind of assessment is more than a mere collection of facts about observable behavior, for variables which cannot be measured in a strictly scientific sense also need to be examined.

The procedures advocated here often differ from those currently being applied, since standardized tests play a smaller role. The use of standardized tests should not be abolished; rather, newer and more appropriate techniques must be designed to measure characteristics which do not lend themselves to the more traditional methods. Such techniques include self-observations of behavior, instruments that point out positive attributes instead of deficiencies, and techniques with a strong element of realism, such as performance tests and simulations. Although evaluations of the resulting data may not employ "scientific" criteria, it is the improved self-knowledge that students derive from the information that counts most.

Assessment programs must be designed *with* students rather than for or about them; therefore, only information that can directly increase students' self-understanding or improve their self-direction need be collected. The primary purpose of many assessment efforts has been to help student affairs workers better understand their "clients." Although this objective is desirable, it has tended to create volumes of information *about* students that is rarely used directly by them. Educators should also consider the present concern for personal privacy, because collecting information and disseminating it to others in the academic community may invade the student's privacy. So what is needed is to teach students how to obtain and use data themselves.

EL CENTRO PROGRAM

The Student Self-Assessment Program at El Centro College, Dallas, Texas, provides self-assessment in conjunction with formal evaluation. The rationale for this one-day lab is basically twofold: to give students the opportunity to look at their own abilities and select their own courses on the basis of their perceptions, and to give students a feeling of community within the college—a feeling that even from the beginning they know some students and faculty members. Once they do exercises planned to accomplish these two objectives, students register for their courses in a relaxed, informal atmosphere.

49

The program involves all full-time incoming freshmen taking twelve or more semester hours and may be spread over six to twelve days, depending on anticipated enrollment. The staff includes ten to twelve professional counselors, ten to twelve peer counselors, one secretary, four persons from the admissions office, and three from the business office. The facilities and equipment they use are twelve classrooms, a registration and assembly area, overhead projectors, test materials, college catalogs, and so on.

Students take a series of four tests which they score themselves. The Nelson Denny Reading Comprehension test determines whether they should go into such courses as history and psychology or into developmental reading courses. The decision to take developmental writing or college English is based on the student's self-perception and scores on a combination of tests—the SCAT Verbal, a writing sample, and the Nelson Denny. Experience has shown that combining the reading test with the others gives a better predictive score than does any one used alone. The Survey of Interpersonal Values is also given, but since there is little time in this one day to discuss its results, students are encouraged to make a personal appointment with a counselor to get this information.

The students record the results of their scores on the Self-Assessment and Course Selection form, which is designed to allow the students' own perceptions of their abilities, their interests, and their high school grades to help determine the level of entry into various courses. The assumption here is that the students' views may be as valid as their test scores and should have some bearing on their course selection.

The staff members guide the students through the self-assessment form, helping them choose a major, find the course requirements for that major, select their courses, and make the schedule for their first semester. As the students work through the form, staff members recommend courses that are in line with their scores and self-perceptions. Although students are not required to follow these recommendations, the majority do. Students are also told about their chances of success as determined by studies of previous groups. However, factors that cannot be measured cause some students to believe that the counselors' recommendations may not fit them.

Assessing Individual Growth

Assessment for student development is a continuing process, not an activity undertaken only when a student enters or leaves college. It should be used in conjunction with goal setting and change strategies to establish an integrated system for encouraging growth. In fact, these three elements interlock in a cyclical process: (1) the student's needs are diagnosed; (2) goals are determined; (3) the student's current level of achievement on a goal-oriented continuum is specified so that appropriate objectives can be established; (4) the strategies needed to achieve the desired goal are outlined; (5) the student's performance is continuously assessed throughout the implementation period; and (6) movement toward or attainment of goals is evaluated. Since the final step can also serve as diagnostic assessment, the process begins once more, continuously moving toward more advanced levels of development.

Today the assessment practitioner is primarily a technician who collects, processes, and interprets data. But in the future, the total relationship with the student will have center stage. Through this association, the student affairs worker becomes aware of the need to assess, identifies what aspects of the student's development would benefit most from evaluation, and clarifies what information is important from the standpoint of different value systems. As the educator models the way to proceed, the student learns how to use it. The informal assessment that is usually part of this relationship will continue to be important, but it will be supplemented by a more systematic approach. Thus, the educator does less interpreting of behavior and provides more descriptive feedback *about* behavior so that the student can establish a sound foundation on which to build. This relationship is also the context in which the privacy issue must be resolved. Each student, in cooperation with a student development educator and in full cognizance of the legal limitations already established, must take responsibility for determining where the need for accurate information ends and where individual rights to privacy begin.

If assessment is to become a significant part of the student

51

development program, five crucial needs must be met. (1) **An adequate** theory relating assessment to the total student development process must be formulated. (2) Both the type and limits of useful information must be specified, since the potential array is infinitely large. (3) The kinds of instruments and techniques referred to earlier are needed; some of these are already available commercially, but others will have to be constructed locally. (4) A strategy for helping students organize, process, and integrate this information with their belief system is needed. (5) Personnel trained in both the theory and mechanics of an assessment program for student development are also required.

RATIONALE

What is it about student development that makes assessment important? As indicated in Chapter One, growing is a cumulative business. Knowledge of an individual's, group's, or organization's present status is a prerequisite to planned change. Two problems have commonly arisen in past programs: students have often been placed in instructional sequences in which they had little or no real interest or they have been assigned to a program before they have the basic skills they need to succeed. As a result, students have often been faced with an uphill battle to survive academically, let alone grow. To offer a series of disconnected programs is not enough. Institutions should provide integrated programs based on a continuum of the skills and concepts needed to master particular subjects or gain certain skills. And students must have the opportunity to determine their current level of development in relation to the requirements and expectations involved.

Assessment is also important because it helps to identify the uniqueness of each individual, who not only differs from others but finds developmental differences within himself or herself. Assessment has the potential to reveal how well he or she is functioning in one or all of the developmental areas.

Since human behavior is a complex yet integrated whole, a multifaceted program has a better chance of providing a good picture of the behavioral interactions as an individual grows. Therefore, a broad array of assessment techniques should be used to gather the comprehensive data that contribute to an understanding of the whole individual.

Assessment helps the growing student in a number of ways. Integrating new information about one's present level of development with one's belief system promotes self-awareness and serves as a base for planning improvements; evaluating growth alternatives improves the likelihood that intelligent decisions will be made; pinpointing the reasons for learning deficiencies increases the ability to overcome obstacles; and determining how much change is taking place provides evidence of progress toward goals. Learning to carry out the whole procedure helps one become a more self-directed individual.

For the student development educator, assessment data can best be used to design effective learning environments. Since change is a function of both the individual and the environment (Walsh, 1973), the educator needs to analyze the relevant characteristics of a given milieu and the impact they have on the individuals who experience them. Using empirical information from assessment, students can be helped to establish propitious conditions, eliminate unfavorable ones, and select the most efficient strategy to promote learning.

DELINEATING USEFUL INFORMATION

The second requirement of an effective program is to help students decide what kinds of information will be most useful to them. The selection of the variables to be measured is determined in part by the student's need for information, by the educator's professional values, by the need for the data to meet certain "scientific" criteria, and by the educator's theoretical position. For example, as Cross (1975) points out, developmentalists would use complex scales to assess the process by which students master specific developmental tasks, humanists would assess goals, such as openness and honesty, using self-assessment procedures, while multidimensionalists would employ personality and attitude inventories to measure what happens to students. Thus, educators apply their values to determine

53

what development *should* take place according to their past experiences with students, their personal developmental process, and the available research delineating what actually happens. This personal viewpoint is fine and inevitable, but a comprehensive assessment program would employ all three theoretical stances in collecting information.

The student's need for information generally arises from four primary sources.

First, entering or leaving an educational experience often stimulates individual assessment because the student must make decisions about available alternatives both within and outside the institution. Orientation programs, for instance, have the potential to go far beyond the traditional effort to help students adjust to their new situation. And departure invariably raises such questions as "Should I go to work?" "Should I continue my education?" "Do I have any marketable skills?" that require careful evaluation. Times of major personal upheaval, which may well include entering or leaving an environment, are also likely to increase the individual's openness to personal change (Hoyt, 1968), and a student development program would, therefore, be wise to capitalize on them.

Second, decisions concerning institutional involvement create opportunities for self-assessment. Before the beginning of each new academic term, students must choose the courses they will take. For some individuals, this necessity creates a need to think again about what career goals they want to pursue, what courses they enjoy, and related matters. Even the requirement to declare an academic major stirs a desire and need to know more about oneself. Other kinds of decisions—whether to live off campus or join certain social groups, for instance—also give students opportunities to learn what assessment is all about.

Third, unmet needs and unsolved problems are a major source of motivation. Difficulties associated with attaining desired study goals, learning to live with others, or deriving a sense of satisfaction from life stimulate students to examine those goals, values, and personal qualities which could help them fulfill their needs and resolve their problems.

Fourth, intervention by others in the campus community may encourage students to investigate specific aspects of their development. For example, a counselor may comment that a student could benefit from clarifying his or her values before making a decision. Or a teacher may ask thought-provoking questions in the classroom. Even a residence hall staff member may suggest that an individual learn leadership skills in order to assist with the hall government. Or a fellow student may exhibit a set of personal values which challenges one's own. Clearly, the student is exposed to many people who stimulate and challenge participation in the process of self-assessment.

Whatever the source of the need for information, the student should be encouraged to examine the emotional or affective aspects of behavior which have often been neglected in traditional assessment programs. Bloom, Hastings, and Madaus (1971) disclose various reasons for the neglect of affective outcomes, including fear of indoctrination, the lack of appropriate tests for measuring intangible variables, the length of time required for attaining affective objectives, and the private character of the information which is not appropriate for formal record-keeping. These are formidable barriers, yet they must be overcome if the goal of developing whole persons is to be achieved.

The first task in assessing this kind of development is to define it in behavioral terms: what actions will yield evidence of the presence or absence of some affective construct in the student? Krathwohl, Bloom, and Masia (1964), in their useful taxonomy of affective educational objectives, portray a hierarchy of action. At first, students are merely aware of or able to perceive a phenomenon, but at the second level, they are willing to attend to it. On level three, they respond with feeling and purpose to the phenomenon, and at the next level individuals organize their behavior and feelings into a conceptual structure. The peak of this hierarchy is reached when this structure becomes a total philosophy. Several methods can be used to determine one's current level of functioning, including projective techniques, the interview, and the semantic differential technique (Osgood, Suci, and Tannenbaum, 1957).

Additional instruments that measure performance other than verbal or written communications alone would be useful.

A program that reveals a commitment to developing the affective and vocational identities of students was proposed for Monmouth College in Illinois and is being applied at the Mara Institute of Technology in Malaysia. It requires a behavioral profile (Who am I?) to be drawn before students establish behavioral objectives (Where am I going?) and strategies (How am I going to get there?). By failing to take this first step, colleges typically lose students, who often graduate without knowing how much growth they have achieved and how self-directed their learning has become.

Entering freshmen have an opportunity to look at three aspects of their development: their academic or cognitive skills, their personal or affective behaviors, and their vocational interests. The instruments administered are the College Qualifications Test, the Kuder Occupational Interest Survey, and the Omnibus Personality Inventory. An assessment specialist discusses the results with students individually and in a developmental group of eight to ten persons. The group gives them a chance to get responses from their peers while they experience the process of self-assessment. Each student also creates a portfolio containing separate profiles of the three developmental areas; a "set" of behavioral objectives consistent with these descriptions; and a plan for attaining personal goals. This portfolio can serve as the basis for reevaluation at any time during the educational experience.

MEASUREMENT TECHNIQUES

A variety of information-gathering devices, including paper-and-pencil instruments, is needed. One of the major tasks for the student development specialist in the future will be to develop instrumentation appropriate for many purposes. Unobtrusive measures usable in real-world situations designed to fit specific local needs must be devised. A corollary task is to prevent the use of poorly constructed, inappropriate, or inaccurate assessment procedures. The development of fair and accurate techniques uncontaminated by sexism, racism, and other biases is a difficult but extremely important goal. The available options should range from a completely subjective approach, such as an unstructured interview, to a highly objective measurement tool like a structured, validated psychological test. The variable being assessed, as well as time limits and other practical considerations, will determine which techniques are most useful. In most cases, an instrument that relates an individual's progress to an absolute performance standard (a "criterion-referenced" measure) is preferable to one that compares him or her to other individuals (a "norm-referenced" measure, such as a typical standardized test).

Since the general purpose of all assessment is to foster the learning of self-evaluation skills, the techniques that are chosen or created should give students an accurate index of their abilities and capacities. Especially good are informal, nontraditional methods which can be used to get a quick evaluation of a specific problem. In addition to the several techniques presented below, other reviews, such as *A Compendium of Assessment Techniques* (Knapp and Sharon, 1975), should be consulted to discover various ways to help individuals learn how to judge their personal levels of development.

Self-Observation. Having the individual use his or her own perceptual skills to examine behavior is the recommended first step in programs for self-improvement, because a person must know what is happening before any effort to change can be effective. Precise records of behavior before and after a strategy is begun increase an individual's awareness of progress. Two recent publications, *Behavioral Self-Control* (Thoresen and Mahoney, 1974) and *Toward a Self-Managed Life Style* (Williams and Long, 1975), give instructions for recording the quantity and circumstances of behavior that needs to be changed. To make sure their self-reports are reliable and valid, individuals should be trained to discriminate, chart, count, record, and analyze both overt and covert behavior. Such training is enhanced by modeling, immediate and accurate feedback, systematic reinforcement, and gradual transfer of recording responsibilities.

Self-observation methods include the use of written records, wrist counters, knitting-stitch counters, bead counters and videotapes. Counting techniques tend to be more accurate when responses are recorded as they occur. Behavior records may comprise simple frequency counts, such as the number of times an interfering gesture was used in speaking; measurements of how long a behavior was manifested, such as the amount of time invested in crying or studying; or examinations of the products of some behavior, such as the number of completed assignments turned in. A graph on which the vertical axis denotes the quantity of behavior (frequency, duration, amount or percentage) and the horizontal axis represents the base line and treatment days often leads to improvement in the behavior under consideration. All these counting methods can be easily used by individuals throughout a change program.

A Behavior-Assessment Scale. A useful tool for evaluating particular levels of achievement is the Student Development Task Inventory (Prince, Miller, and Winston, 1974). The nine tasks assessed are both global (developing autonomy, mature interpersonal relationships, and purpose) and specific (developing emotional autonomy, tolerance, and mature career plans, for example). The SDTI provides examples of the kinds of behavior that students could be expected to demonstrate when they have satisfactorily accomplished developmental tasks. Since the inventory is self-scored, it gives respondents immediate information about the extent to which their behavior conforms to these criteria.

After completing and scoring the inventory, the student and a student development educator should talk about the meaning and use of the results. Open-ended questions in an unstructured interview help the student clarify specific responses on the inventory, identify inconsistencies, and obtain a better understanding of his or her present developmental status. In addition, students find these data useful for both identifying their needs and establishing appropriate goals.

Values Clarification Techniques. Hall (1973a, 1973b), Simon and his coauthors (1972), and Simon (1973) present numerous strategies for helping people examine their values. One exercise which could be used as a summary technique crystallizes new learning by helping individuals focus on their reactions to life. This approach is one way of processing experiences so they become usable. Students are asked to complete these sentence stems:

I learned that I . . .
I relearned that I . . .
I became aware that I . . .
I was surprised that I . . .
I was disappointed that I . . .
I see that I need to . . .

Participation in such exercises tends to give the student additional self-assessment data which could be used to plan future actions as well as to better understand previous behavior.

Physiological Feedback or Biofeedback. These systems present instantaneous information to an individual about what is presently occurring inside—for example, muscle tension, heart rate, temperature, or brain waves—using visual or auditory electrophysiological measurement devices. Voluntary self-regulation of these processes can result in voluntary control of psychological states, such as test anxiety, insomnia, stress, and irrational fears. Successful use of these techniques can have a broader impact on a person's sense of worth, relevance, and autonomy (Danskin and Walters, 1973). Additional sources of information on biofeedback training are Barber and others (1971) and Stoyva and others (1971).

Counseling Outcome Inventory. Hill (1975) presents a unique way to get the student involved in assessment by constructing an inventory during a counseling session. In the first step, the counselor asks the student to specify about fifteen characteristics, qualities, or descriptors which the student feels are most important. For example, the counselor could say, "Tell me how you would like to be described," and the student might respond, "I would like to be more self-confident." This exploration phase typically requires some time because the student finds it difficult to look at himself or herself this way. Next, the counselor helps the student specify at least one behavioral "anchor point" for each of the descriptors. As a behavioral anchor point for more self-confidence, the student might specify that he or she would make fewer negative self-statements about himself or herself. This base not only gives a clear goal to work toward but is a valuable reference for subsequent evaluations. In step three, students rank the ten top descriptors and then rate their possession of the ten qualities on a scale from −3 to +3. For each item, the rank is multiplied by the self-rating to obtain a weighted score of the student's perceptions. The added scores represent the student's overall evaluation of his or her present functioning. Counselors have reported that the COI proved to be a valuable aid in specifying what the student expected from a counseling relationship and that it reduced ambiguity concerning what had occurred during the session. The *process* of the measure allows the student and counselor to develop an understanding of where the student stands. Variations of the COI could be used in a number of developmental areas such as the assessment step which precedes goal setting and selection of a change strategy. Various self-ratings could also be taken while the student was implementing the plan, and the initial inventory could be used again during a final evaluation session.

Student Development Transcript. Brown and Citrin (1975) have suggested a student development transcript with a number of useful purposes. For one, the student's awareness that a developmental chart was being maintained might stimulate self-assessment, give credence to noncognitive activities, and promote awareness of the broad range of possible goals and areas for personal development. There are three possible formats: (1) an experiential checklist; (2) a competency-based checklist, and (3) a portfolio. The experiential transcript presents a list of items (such as activities and experiences developed by the student alone or in collaboration with an advisor) intended to move the student along a developmental path. Included are academic courses, organized extra-classroom programs, and specific skills to be developed. A competency-based transcript contains a list of abilities specified by the student and clearly delineates the tasks that are to be completed to demonstrate competence. For the portfolio, the student, with the assistance of an advisor, compiles a variety of testimonials, products, experience records, and other items which portray what he or she has been doing.

Directed Discussion. Alverno College assesses the development of an understanding of contemporary events, social interactions, and the speaking aspect of communications by having four to six students sit down with a trained discussion leader and engage in an oral exchange. A four-member assessment team evaluates their performance in specific terms and reaches consensus regarding their level of achievement. Such simulations provide a way to see whether the students can use newly acquired learning in an unfamiliar situation; they also give the students an opportunity to test out their new abilities in a relatively nonthreatening context. Through this experience, students gain an altogether different type of data from the observers' comments on their skill at managing relationships.

APPLYING ASSESSMENT INFORMATION

Of course, understanding and positive development do not flow automatically from information alone. The core of the assessment process, for the student affairs worker, is to help students figure out what to examine and decide how they will evaluate and use the resulting data. If these steps are well taken, students will comprehend the feedback they receive and be able to integrate new information with their present views of themselves. Because several sources already describe feedback procedures (Anastasi, 1968; Tyler, 1971; Goldman, 1971), actions and attitudes that encourage self-direction will be the focus here.

(1) Recognize the student's present capacities, because knowledge of and pride in accomplishments are powerful forces urging him or her to continue growing.

(2) Focus on individual worth and development. Although comparative data are still useful, an overemphasis on them can create damaging labels such as "remedial student" and "compensatory program." Help the student use the assessment information to develop an honest appreciation for his or her unique individuality and abilities.

(3) Encourage students to work for their own positive goals and not to change behavior that someone else thinks should be corrected. A positive outlook has top priority, and the student must be given responsibility for making developmental decisions.

(4) Describe behavior instead of interpreting it. "Experts" often try to explain behavior without completely understanding what it is, and their interpretations draw heavily on their own value

61

system. Descriptive feedback permits students to use their own values in judging their behavior, especially if they have had some practice in clarifying what they believe and prize.

(5) Show that values play a legitimate role in assessment. Individuals need to recognize that both the instruments they use and the decisions they make about what to measure are based on subjective considerations.

(6) Adopt relevant and understandable feedback units instead of such things as letter grades or scores on scales with mystifying labels which may or may not relate to what is being evaluated. Profiles of behavior, descriptions of behavior in everyday language, specific information about the frequency or duration of actions, and other measurements that will increase understanding and decrease confusion should be developed with students from available data.

(7) Avoid isolated, "one-shot" assessments. The student development educator must help students learn how to use the information gained through evaluation to set goals and objectives, to design methods to improve their behavior or develop new skills, and to test out alternatives for enhancing growth and development.

(8) View assessment results as tentative. As new samples of behavior are observed and new inferences formulated, the picture of an individual changes. To see earlier evaluations as immutable is to deny that development is change. How often have test scores or records of behavior dogged students over the years even though subsequent data reveal change?

(9) Use a variety of techniques instead of a single procedure. The combination of self-observation reports and information generated by interaction with another can direct change better than either approach alone. Although information provided by the individual is primary, the value of external evaluation should not be overlooked.

(10) Take responsibility for clearly transmitting the elements of the assessment process to others and for teaching them how to use these elements effectively. Practice in applying the process to a variety of living situations, including recreational, academic, and social activities, should be promoted and reinforced. Self-directed

development rests on the ability to identify one's own behavior and determine the type of change desired (Goshko, 1973).

Establishing a sound relationship between the student or group and the student affairs worker is the first order of business. This association can be basically prescriptive or developmental (Crookston, 1972a). In the prescriptive relationship, the educator judges the student's abilities, using past records and scores to predict future behavior. Clearly, students have a passive, lesser role in this context; since they are considered immature, irresponsible, and often incapable of making sound decisions, they are thought to require close supervision. The educator also assumes that the student's primary goals are achieving a high grade, gaining credit for a course, or obtaining a degree in order to realize a certain level of income. In the developmental relationship, on the other hand, the equal participants focus on the student's positive potential and on the rewards of personal growth, self-fulfillment, and human commitment. The student is seen as a maturing individual who is able to share the responsibility for initiating the behavior that is expected to evolve within the relationship. The goals of this collaboration are openness, acceptance, trust, sharing of data, and cooperative problem solving, decision making and evaluation.

Although the assessment process which they engage in together is continuous, it can be usefully analyzed in three steps, called the initial, formative, and summative stages. Each stage has its particular purposes, techniques, and reporting methods.

Initial Stage. Step one is to help students learn about and describe the behavior, attitudes, and abilities, such as verbal and nonverbal skills, that characterize their present social, physical, emotional, and intellectual growth. Traditional tests of cognitive mastery are still a useful part of this diagnosis because they can be used to place students in programs or courses for which they have the necessary skills. But the student also needs to know about such things as his or her degree of personal autonomy and how well he or she relates to others. This information can help determine readiness for learning experiences that are just as relevant as intellectual tasks to success in college and life. For instance, could he or she benefit now from a self-awareness group, a leadership skills workshop, or an assertiveness training program? Placement, then, is one of the primary functions of assessment from the beginning.

A secondary activity is discovering the causes of particular problems or learning blocks. Actually, such an analysis can be undertaken whenever the student sees a need for it, but it may well be started in the initial stage. The instruments used to make these evaluations are purposely designed to measure general skills and traits. Some personal abilities may best be assessed initially with behavior inventories, self-rating scales, or adjective checklists, which help students place themselves along a developmental continuum without being compared to others. Another way to avoid early comparisons is to examine individual items on standardized instruments. Eventually, however, some students will probably want to get a picture of their strengths and weaknesses in relation to some norm group—persons of the same age or personality type, perhaps. Standardized instruments are available for this purpose.

The first report of information is usually an individual profile of the student's cognitive, affective, or psychomotor characteristics. Real-ideal discrimination score profiles and lists of personal interests or needs are sometimes provided, also. All these data are then used by the student and the educator to create and set in motion a systematic plan for personal development.

Formative Stage. As its name implies, the next step is taken while students are forming certain behavior patterns and thus is not limited to the beginning or end of a given growth process (Scriven, 1967; Bloom, Hastings, and Madeus, 1971). Since the primary function of formative assessment is to give students feedback as they move through a learning experience, the data it produces can be used to determine specific objectives for that part of the task yet to be mastered. Formative assessment is particularly important when the learning sequence is hierarchial, requiring achievement of increasingly complex skills. To be most effective, therefore, formative

64

assessment must be frequent and flexible so that the student's goals and strategies can be modified or changed immediately, if necessary. In this way, assessment is a means to individualize learning, to pace the student's efforts, and to reward or reinforce motivation to succeed.

The measuring devices used during this stage are intended to locate in relatively precise fashion where a student is within a given learning sequence. And thus they analyze separate components of a large domain of behavior. Although the need to give feedback as quickly as possible sometimes interferes with the desire to meet strict "scientific" criteria, the information produced by formative assessment is just as valuable to the student as any other evaluative data. The form of the feedback is also important. Since a total score is often not very meaningful, the student affairs worker should show students what their responses mean in terms of mastery and non-mastery of the skills and content measured by the instrument. Thus students find out whether they are reaching or failing to achieve each of their objectives. Because the learner must progress from simpler to more complex behavior, continuous formative assessment and feedback are needed to develop efficiently.

Summative Stage. The last kind of assessment measures how well the student has succeeded, over an extended period, in achieving preestablished goals; that is, growth must be empirically demonstrated. Summative assessment differs from other types in that its data are more general; and it is performed at the end of a program or a term to evaluate the strategy used to bring about change, to profile changes which took place, or to certify competence in a given skill.

Many of the same instruments that were used during the initial assessment are administered again. The familiar pretest-posttest research design is an example of combining initial and summative assessments for purposes of evaluating research or programs. Most any technique that can identify the degree of accomplishment achieved by an individual, group, or organization is potentially useful in this third stage. Results are usually reported as a total score, and comparative scores are often shown. The findings may also be

65

used to evaluate how well different change strategies worked for different types of students. And finally, summative assessment can be treated as the first step in a new round of the developmental cycle.

ENVIRONMENTAL ASSESSMENT

Thus far, the person as the determiner of behavior has been the primary focus of this discussion. But the setting of change is also important, and an assessment of the relevant characteristics of the environment can be most valuable to a developing student. Such information is especially needed when a student is making decisions about entering a particular milieu.

Several approaches may be taken to analyzing the environment. Walsh (1973) reviews and contrasts five theories of person-environment interaction. The first of these, Barker's theory (1968), emphasizes only the environmental component. His "behavior settings" concept, based on data obtained from a Behavior Setting Survey, supports the notion that there is a relationship between the number of people in a given environment and what takes place in it.

The subculture model describes the environment in terms of the attitudes, values, behaviors, and roles of its members. One typology (Clark and Trow, 1966) identifies the four primary student subcultures as academic, nonconformist, collegiate, and vocational. Peterson (1968) used this theoretical model in the College Student Questionnaire to determine the relationship between the student's identification with subcultural ideas and identification with the college. Thus, the environment is described not by its members' perceptions of it but by the characteristics of those in that environment.

Holland defines environments according to their resemblance to six personality types—realistic, investigative, artistic, social, enterprising, and conventional—which he has developed from responses to the Vocational Preference Inventory (Holland, 1965), the Self Directed Search (Holland, 1970), and scales from items on the Strong Vocational Interest Blank (Campbell and Holland, 1972). These environments are further described by using the Environmental Assessment Technique (Astin and Holland, 1961).

Assessing Individual Growth

The environment is seen by Stern (1970) as having certain "presses" or characteristic demands it makes on its members. Thus, the environment is defined by their collective perceptions as manifested through four indices: the College Characteristics Index, the Evening College Characteristics Index, the High School Characteristics Index, and the Organizational Climate Index. Persons are represented as being in certain "need states" in which they tend to perform particular actions. Cohen (1966) completed a factor analysis of need and press variables in fifty-five institutions and then identified five composite cultures—expressive, intellectual, protective, vocational, and collegiate.

The last of the theories explored by Walsh is that of Pervin (1967), who measures perceptions of the environment using the Transactional Analysis of Personality and Environment (TAPE). Individuals, defined by their own self-perceptions, find transactions with the environment to be most satisfying when there is congruence between their personal characteristics and those of the milieu.

Another assessment tool that has the potential to enlighten students concerning their environmental setting was developed by Smail, DeYoung, and Moos (1974). The University Residence Environment Scale (URES) systematically evaluates the similarities and differences among the perceived psychosocial climates of a variety of student living groups, including residence halls, fraternities, and sororities. It describes and measures student-student and student-staff relationships, as well as the organizational structure of the living group. The psychometric details of the development and makeup of URES are discussed in Moos and Gerst (1972).

Still another useful instrument is the College and University Environment Scales, (Pace, 1969), consisting of one hundred statements about the intellectual-social-cultural climate of the college as perceived by students. The five dimensions of the scale are: *practicality*, the degree to which personal status and practical benefits are emphasized in the college environment; *community*, the degree to which the campus is friendly, cohesive, and group-oriented; *awareness*, the degree of emphasis on self-understanding, personal identity, and personal involvement in the world's problems; *propriety*, the degree to which politeness, protocol, and consideration are em-

67

phasized; and *scholarship,* the degree to which high academic achievement is evidenced by concern for scholarship and ideas.

Whatever approach is used to describe the institutional environment, the information should be made directly available to students, as well as others concerned with the campus setting. Students should be active participants in determining what facets of their milieu they would most like to know about.

An example of a program that employs environmental analysis is the Environmental Assessment Phone Survey, developed by the Consultation Unit of the Student Counseling Center at Illinois State University in Normal. The program is noteworthy in that students assume the responsibility for finding out how their peers feel about various aspects of college life. Its specific goals are (1) to more closely identify student needs and problems; (2) to acquire specifics about the impact of a selected number of environmental elements on students; and (3) to serve as a catalyst for new programs.

A variety of people and departments contribute their efforts to the survey. Seventy-two student paraprofessionals (paras), selected, employed, trained, and supervised by the Student Counseling Center, generate many of the raw items during brainstorming sessions on "What factors in the environment affect students?" Faculty members in sociology are consulted concerning survey techniques. Staff members from Institutional Research and Computer Operations select the random sample (2 percent of the student body, or 280 students) and analyze the data.

Each para conducts four structured fifteen-minute interviews during a ten-day period. Eighteen questions from four categories are asked on ecology; programs, politics, and procedures; inhabitant characteristics; and psychosocial "climate." The questioning follows a regular format: (1) the respondent is asked for a positive, negative, or neutral reaction (a valence statement); (2) the paraprofessional asks how strongly (positive) (negative) (neutral) he or she feels; (3) the questioner probes for an environmental referent ("What specifically . . . leads you to feel this way?").

In the second phase of this environmental assessment approach, the paras report the results of their phone survey findings.

Every two weeks throughout the academic year they complete an Environmental Assessment Inventory. The summary of their responses produces an "environmental baseline map" of the campus which gives the Consultation Unit staff ample data to examine for emerging environmental trends. When an item stands out clearly as an important factor—be it positive or negative in nature—closer examination is made. For instance, small-group interviews might be held with the paras to explore the particular referents involved. It could be found that students are having difficulty taking advantage of a campus service because outsiders are interfering or because there are too few staff members to provide it. This concrete information can then result in a consultation between the students and various decision makers, from top-level administrators to individual faculty and staff members. The aim is to shape the campus so that it supports, instead of hinders, student development as much as possible. One positive result has been the establishment of campus environmental workshops for faculty members to familiarize them with assessment findings.

As a result of using this "ecomapping barometer" of campus environmental press, the Consultation Unit can function much more effectively than would be the case if they needed to wait until the "lid blew off" to take action. For a more detailed treatment of how to create better people-oriented environments through assessment strategies, see Conyne (1975) and Aulepp and Delworth (1976) as well.

THE ASSESSMENT CENTER AND ITS STAFF

A special center, established as a part of a student development program, would serve an important function by consolidating assessment activities within the institution and using its resources to evaluate many different facets of student learning. Faculty members, administrators, student affairs workers, and students would contribute to the solution of assessment problems. Effective individual and institutional functioning would be measured with a combination of techniques, including interviews, paper-and-pencil tests, and simulations.

A major task of the center would be teaching faculty, students, and staff how to carry out the assessment process. To fulfill this responsibility, student development staff members need the following abilities and characteristics:

• Skill in using both test and nontest techniques as well as an understanding of the potential and limitations of any data collected.

• A sound background in instrument construction in order to develop new methods for meeting special requirements.

• Ability to organize and develop an assessment program in which data collection is based on real needs and purposes.

• Skill in test selection, administration, and interpretation.

• Willingness to use nontraditional assessment techniques.

• Capacity for sharing descriptive feedback information with individuals, groups, and organizations.

• Skill at motivating others to use assessment data in conjunction with goal setting and planning.

• Ability to conduct an assessment process without preconceived assumptions about student behavior based on sex, age, race, or cultural heritage.

• Competence in handling assessment without infringing on a student's right to privacy.

• Skill at assessing their own behavior and development.

• Capacity to identify and control personal needs which might limit their ability to facilitate growth in others, for example, the need to foster student dependence.

• Ability to model effective personal assessment behavior.

Not all student affairs staff members will be specialists in assessment, but all should recognize its important role in the student development program. All should exhibit mature self-evaluation behavior in their own lives.

SUMMARY AND IMPLICATIONS

Why is assessment for student development important? It is intimately bound to an understanding of human development; it balances a new emphasis on affective behavior with the traditional attention to cognitive abilities; it stresses positive growth instead of remediation; and, most of all, its aim is to produce individuals who can design and carry out plans to change their lives on their own without depending on others to do it for them.

These functions and goals make increased demands on student affairs workers to coordinate a systematic assessment program, to construct accurate and unbiased instruments to fit local needs, and to develop relationships with students which will help them find out where they want to go and take responsibility for getting there. Many types of assessment activity will be carried out concurrently on the college campus, and the student development educator must strive to make sure the individual parts contribute effectively to the whole program.

Additional research on useful techniques for evaluating both individuals and their environments is essential. A simple set of methods will not be adequate to examine complex human behavior. Nevertheless, attempts must be made to develop instruments that can be easily used by students, faculty members, and student affairs staff alike in varied assessment activities.

In addition to the characteristics mentioned above, the features of an assessment program which would contribute significantly to student development include the following: (1) a formal mechanism (such as a campus assessment center) to coordinate a systematic program; (2) student development educators who are good at assessment and who have direct, continuing relationships with students; (3) the capacity to engage in initial, formative (process), and summative (product) assessment simultaneously; (4) adherence to the general procedure of delineating, obtaining, and processing information; (5) and a well-organized educational program to teach students, faculty members, administrators, and student affairs workers the elements of assessment and how to use them. These features, which have often been noticeably lacking in many programs, are needed if assessment is to make significant contributions to student development.

Chapter 4

꙰꙰꙰꙰꙰꙰꙰꙰

Instruction

Student affairs workers have discovered that effective practice of their art with contemporary students must include approaches that go far beyond those required in the privacy of a counseling office. Administrators and faculty members have increasingly recognized that the goals of general education probably will never be achieved by continued preoccupation with subject matter alone. Other methods are important in helping a student learn how to function in a world of accelerating change. With this need in mind, the three strategies for change that appear to be most comprehensive and utilitarian—instruction, consultation, and milieu management—are discussed here and in the next two chapters.

Instruction

As part of a holistic student development program, instruction gives students both knowledge and practice at applying what they learn. It seeks to integrate affective learning and cognitive subjects to produce what has been called confluent (Brown, 1971) or humanistic (Weinstein and Fantini, 1970) or psychological education (Ivey and Alschuler, 1973). Developmental instruction recognizes that people learn in a variety of ways: from the body and its senses, from aesthetic perception, and from intuition and imagination, as well as through rational processes (Change in Liberal Education, 1974). Instead of focusing solely on traditional subjects, this kind of teaching tries to show students the interconnectedness of human experience.

All of these aims and functions suggest that the educational dimensions of many nontraditional activities should be incorporated into the regular curriculum as legitimate academic concerns. By considering these out-of-class developmental experiences as worthy subjects for instruction, we can make them available to all students. Formal teacher-learner relationships can help students grow as persons, add to their self-knowledge, improve their interpersonal effectiveness, and help them function better in groups.

As Crookston (1973) puts it, the teaching of human development includes any experience in which a teacher interacts with students individually or collectively that contributes to individual, group, or community growth and development. He sees the entire academic community and beyond as an environment in which teaching and learning take place, whether or not it results in formal academic credit.

Brown (1972) suggests that student affairs workers take on the role of college professor and establish practical courses in human relations which relate theories to skill development and personal growth. In a somewhat less direct instructional role, the student development educator can be a member of a teaching team in existing courses that lend themselves to the practice of broad personal learning. In fact, any kind of developmental ability or skill that can be taught, either formally or informally, could potentially be the subject of a class.

In *New Approaches to College Student Development,* Tollefson (1975) identified three major clusters of curricular opportunities that indicate a trend toward implanting student development in academic life: courses in human development or life-style planning; atypical methods, such as independent study or experiential learning; and classes with nontraditional (and previously unacceptable) contents, such as how to confront and cope with politicians, how to prepare for death, and other topics related to a student's personal purposes and goals.

Clearly, then, instruction for student development is not seen as something to be tacked onto the curriculum but as an integral part of it. In some cases, this aim can be achieved by emphasizing developmental goals in traditional courses, such as psychology and biology, and by using student-centered techniques, such as discussion groups, in many courses. In other cases, new offerings are needed. These should give academic credit for both structured and unstructured experiences that foster affective as well as cognitive growth. Practicums in human relations, leadership training sessions, or decision-making programs should be readily available to students who need them.

THEORETICAL POSITION

The following statements are derived from our general views of human development. (1) Any developmental task which can be taught systematically is a suitable subject for academic instruction. (2) When students have opportunities to learn that development occurs in stages, they can use this knowledge to define what development ought to be and thereby set their own goals for learning (Sprinthall and Erickson, 1974). (3) A productive synthesis of the cognitive and affective components of growth is essential. (4) Since development requires experiment and practice, a desired behavior must be conceptualized, tried out, and digested. The feedback from an organized instructional approach can assist this process (Lenton, 1974).

When developing the potential of the whole person is the

74

goal, it follows that the fragmentation of traditional courses should be replaced by a unified curriculum. When the student, not the subject matter alone, is the focus of instruction, programs and materials should be arranged hierarchically so that the student can master them in logical steps. In this context, the student must accept equal responsibility for how and what he or she learns. One way for students to develop this sense of responsibility is to undertake independent learning in a variety of "real" situations—on the campus, in residence halls, in the larger community—where they can work toward predetermined objectives.

The student and teacher strive together to create a humane learning environment in which the student can understand his or her feelings and translate them into rational action (Crookston, 1973). For them, the purpose of instruction, then, is to provide and receive information in forms that serve the student's personal objectives rather than to convert the student into an instrument for serving the goals of society (Tollefson, 1975).

To be effective, all the personal, ethical, aesthetic, and philosophical learning provided by developmental instruction must be systematically integrated with the student's cognitive structure. So direct experience is balanced by readings, writing assignments, and discussions. When experiential activities are introduced into existing courses, they are intended to help the students accomplish developmental tasks, not just improve their learning of the subject matter or make the classes enjoyable or productive.

INTEGRATED PROGRAMS

An example of a course that united process and content was entitled "Psychological Growth for Women" (Sprinthall and Erickson, 1974). In this practicum-seminar for teen-age girls, the students interviewed girls and women of all ages to understand the tasks of female development at different stages. The seminar sessions helped the students further reflect on and integrate their field experience. They read current articles on sexual stereotyping, examined language and inequality, and looked at the roles of women portrayed in literary works. Most important, they began to explore, in small group discussions, their own emerging choices and personal growth. In this way, the women were continuously connecting the interview data, works of literature, and their self-examination.

Another exemplary program is the Awareness Series at Virginia Commonwealth University in Richmond. Several courses on personal and organizational development are supplemented by topical workshops and retreats. Following are catalog descriptions of three offerings in the series.

> "On Being a Woman." Many women have learned to dampen their most powerful potentialities and have thereby lost them. Women have often been conditioned to accept male and female role stereotypes which are restrictive and limit their individual growth. The goal of the workshop is to help each woman become more aware of her individual strengths and to facilitate more creative choices. Understanding and accepting other women as well as ourselves can provide for a warmth and closeness which may be a highly fulfilling experience. This workshop is limited to thirty women and is scheduled for Friday, 7–10 p.m., and Saturday, 9:30 a.m.–10 p.m.
>
> "Life Planning and Values." Many people, through a variety of previous experiences, have identified within themselves a process which asks, "How can I incorporate my personal awareness into daily living? What is realistic for me to do with my life? Where can I make meaningful changes?" Life planning is designed to provide a framework for each person to set his or her goals and formulate a plan of action with the support and reality-testing of fellow participants. This experience is not aimed at vocational counseling, but at one's personal priorities in terms of time, energy, work commitment, and values. Enrollment is limited to thirty participants. The workshop will be held Friday, 7–10 p.m., and Saturday, 9:30 a.m.–10 p.m.
>
> "Education of Self." This three-credit class, EDU 471/571E, is designed primarily to assist participants in

76

exploring personal identity (Who am I?), individual power and authority (How do I influence others? How do others influence me?), responsibility (How am I sensitive to myself and how do I respond to others?) and connectedness (How do I relate to ideas, people, and groups?). The emphasis of the course is on learning how to learn about yourself and others, the methodology utilized is based on experiential learning theory, and the focus is on maximizing group interaction and individual responsibility for personal learning. This course is not for people who are seeking counseling. It is for people who find learning about themselves and others a genuinely fascinating experience and who are open to experimenting with new behaviors. This course is highly recommended as a prerequisite to EDU 432/532E, Group and Interpersonal Relationships.

The program provides for all members of the VCU community both short- and long-term opportunities to increase their awareness. The staff believes that people have the power to grow, to relate authentically, to actualize inherent potentials, to become more aware of themselves and others—and enjoy that new perception — and to respond to others in a caring way. The release of these personal powers is the expected outcome of the awareness series.

While some didactic instruction takes place, most learning is the result of group interaction and collaboration. Participants are continually encouraged to identify and use all possible resources, especially their fellow participants. Any changes in the total program or its parts are made by the whole staff, sometimes with the help of participants. Additions and deletions reflect the needs of the students and the availability of resources.

Although the program is staffed primarily by student affairs workers, other faculty members, students, and external personnel are used to guide particular experiences. A variety of facilities such as classrooms, small group rooms, dance studios, retreat sites, and churches house the activities.

Participant evaluation reports are requested for all courses, workshops, and retreats. These include journals, "I learned . . ." statements, and midterm and final self-evaluation reports. Procedures for assessing behavioral change and the transfer of learning are being developed. All these techniques are used to help the participants take responsibility for their own learning. "With a little help from their friends"—staff members, their fellow students— and further topical workshops and credit courses, the participants develop individual objectives and begin to act on them.

The current emphasis on individualizing instruction is very much in accord with our views of developmental teaching. To manifest this ideal is not easy, but Eisele (1973) proposes four tasks that could help to make it a reality. Although many of his proposals recapitulate earlier comments, they bear repeating in the context of instruction. The first job is to find out what the learner already knows and what he or she needs or wants to find out. Clearly, the kind of assessment discussed in the last chapter would be useful here. The teacher begins with a picture of what a "successful" student would be able to do after completing the course. Then, using the information derived from the determination of each learner's achievements and aptitudes, plans for learning experiences that will produce as many of those successes as possible are made by the student and teacher.

The next step is defining appropriate objectives that can be mastered by students in measurable ways. Negotiation between the teacher and the student should ensure that they are working toward the same ends and that the teacher does not plan to teach "old stuff" or overly difficult material.

Step three is to design suitable instructional strategies. The teaching-learning process is so labeled because there are many ways to teach and to learn (Parker, 1973). Some content is best imparted through a lecture, and some requires direct experience, just as some students prefer to hear lectures, others like discussions, and yet others find that direct experience is the only way to learn. The methods selected should integrate both content and process, both affective and cognitive objectives. Each class session, therefore, should try to balance thinking and practice.

Finally, evaluation, as expected, wraps up the sequence. Judgments must be made not only about the students' progress but about the effectiveness of instruction—in effect, the former determines the latter. Grades will no doubt enter the picture here, but evaluation should basically be considered a means to assess instruction rather than to certify the student. So questions such as "What did I do that made it easier for you (the student) to learn?" should come into play. Another aspect of evaluation is finding out whether students can transfer their learning to different situations.

El Centro Program. A number of liberal arts colleges have been experimenting with new developmentally oriented courses, particularly for freshmen and sophomores. These include life-planning workshops, seminars on family planning, and training for reducing examination anxiety. But one or two isolated classes cannot compose the critical mass necessary to bring about important changes. A series of comprehensive and integrated behavioral science courses are needed, such as those provided in the Human Development Curriculum of El Centro College in Dallas. In this well-developed program, courses are designed to promote growth both within and among students. Classroom activities allow them to seek answers to the important human questions they bring with them and to examine their own values, beliefs, attitudes, and abilities.

The program has some unusual characteristics. It serves the entire student body, as well as any faculty members who wish to share this experience with students. The classes, which are usually limited to eighteen participants, are offered by a professional person (such as a counselor) who is qualified to lead group experiences. Students receive three semester-hours' credit for completing a course —most courses are offered for the full sixteen-week semester. Students may take any or all of the series, and they usually find that their credits can be transferred to area colleges and universities. The following brief course descriptions give examples of the instructional techniques that are used.

"HD 106—Personal and Social Growth" is a seminar in which students might give oral book reports, invite a guest person (such as a psychologist) to class, and use audiovisuals—films on drugs or race, for example. In "HD 105—Interpersonal Relations," students might go through a series of nonverbal exercises, receive some group encounter experience, or be asked to do some intensive internalization and then share their feelings openly. "HD 107—Leadership Behavior" takes a lecture-seminar approach. Students may be asked to cooperate in preparing a group project on a specific aspect of leadership or to participate in various simulation-learning exercises on decision making. The instructor lectures on various leadership or management principles. In "HD 104—Career Development," self-tests are used. Students may be asked to go through a packet of instructions aimed at classifying career choices, to pursue some information and prepare a report at the College Career Center, or to take part in group discussions on careers.

The role of the faculty member in these classes varies somewhat. Many of the twenty instructors utilize various communication and sensitivity exercises, while others stress discussions or, particularly in HD 107, lectures. Students are expected to earn a grade by completing reading assignments, attending classes, and meeting various other requirements. In their anticipated role, they are also expected to enjoy a class learning/working relationship with their instructor, feel free to discuss things that are important to them, such as God, hate, sex, or happiness, and be responsible for their own actions and behaviors.

Several instruments are used to help students assess their current job interests, study habits, and listening abilities and to give them some ideas about what kinds of abilities they want to develop. These instruments include the Cognitive Style Mapping Inventory, the Sixteen Personality Factor, Permenter's Self-Sufficiency Inventory, and various exercises for clarifying values and for revealing the potential of individual past experiences.

The evaluation process is a multifaceted operation. Each semester students evaluate the instruction they have received. This report is then used by the division chairperson to improve instruction. Instructors also rate the chairperson on whether he or she is providing enough significant leadership and useful strategies to keep the program in top professional form. In addition, an informal evaluation occurs in monthly staff meetings when various differences, problems, and successes are aired and discussed by the staff. Administrators evaluate the program's budget, student feedback, and support from non-HD faculty. Students are asked several times each semester if they feel they are obtaining worthwhile learning experiences.

A study conducted on the results of completing part or all of the HD curriculum revealed that: students' gradepoint averages were higher than when they began; students tended to persist in college; and students clarified their career choices, learned they were competent, and learned it pays both personal and professional dividends to be human.

Finding scientific ways to measure the success of human development classes has often been difficult, but in 1972, as part of its program preparation, El Centro surveyed ninety colleges providing these kinds of courses. The survey revealed the following: (1) all respondents said their HD program helped improve the self-concept of students; (2) 80 percent said their HD program increased the employability of students; (3) 70 percent said their HD courses can be transferred for credit; (4) 77 percent said evidence led them to believe that HD courses helped curtail student dropouts; and (5) a significant percentage said they received community approval for their HD course.

"*Self and the Society.*" Courses can also be originated by students. At the University of Texas at Austin, a president of the student body felt that student leaders would be better members of faculty-student committees if they were more familiar with the university power structure. As a result, a seminar called "Self and the Society" was designed to give students a better understanding of that governance structure, of the individuals currently involved in it, and of how the individual student could best relate to the university. Although some faculty members and student affairs staff members helped make the original plans, student government personnel still think of the course as "theirs." The course was first offered for no credit, but because of student interest and requests, credit was later established.

As currently constituted, the seminar is a three-credit, upper-division, pass-fail course offered in the Division of General and Comparative Studies. It meets weekly for two and a half hours. After a lecture by a different individual each week, the class continues with discussions, case studies, role-playing, and other learning experiences. Enrollment is limited to twenty-four, and the class tends to attract students from many areas of the campus who participate in various kinds of activities and who want to be involved in decision-making. The teaching team comprises an instructor, who acts as continuing coordinator and facilitator, and a graduate assistant who helps with planning and discussion.

Some of the specific outcomes expected from the seminar are: undergraduates who are better informed about higher education in general and particularly on this campus; a cadre of students from which appointments to faculty-student committees can be made; a formalized structure for discussions on campus issues by individuals who are involved in them; and a file of student studies of various aspects of the university, which are an important contribution to the university archives.

Student evaluations are called for twice during the semester: at midterm, students write a short reaction to the course thus far and make suggestions for improvement, and at the end they fill out a questionnaire. To test student reaction to a specific speaker (regent, executive officer, faculty member), an opinion rating form is occasionally used before and after the lecture.

The resource staff changes as the need requires, but some university officials have become regular presenters. Most students have some particular topic they wish to investigate. Recently one student worked to get approval by the athletic council for a wrestling team to participate in NCAA competition, while another headed a student government committee that requested an extra study day between the end of classes and the beginning of exams. Even though the committee did all the "right" things in taking this request through the system, the request was denied. Nevertheless, the student reported that the experience had been positive. Another student was chairperson of a student government group that staged a rock concert attended by some eighty thousand. And a fourth student surveyed women living in residence halls to get their opinions of the Student Health Center and developed a report with recommendations.

Inserting Developmental Goals in the Existing Curriculum: The Tandem Approach. Perhaps the most difficult instructional strategy is getting current courses to incorporate developmental aims. Faculty members and student affairs workers should collaborate to reduce the separation between personal growth and academic learning. One technique is to have a student development educator take responsibility for teaching psychological units within existing courses. The introduction of human relations training into teacher preparation programs is an example.

Another is the Tandem Approach used at Oakton Community College in Morton Grove, Illinois. Here, two instructors develop two courses that share a common theme, such as values, or are directed toward a certain population, such as women returning to school. The two courses are taught consecutively, the same students are registered in both sections, and both instructors participate in both sections. A sample course has the following characteristics:

I: General Description and Approach. This course will explore human communications with an emphasis on writing. It is designed to help students overcome the feeling that they cannot write or that what they have to say is not worth reading or hearing. Within the honest supportive atmosphere of the Human Potential Seminar, a fresh exploration of participants as communicators will take place.

II: Method. An environment in which interpersonal communications can be developed, explored, and understood will be created. Reading, writing, being together, using individual experiences, classroom transactions, and personal discoveries, will be the primary methods used. Classroom activities will investigate how persons behave as they communicate. Students as well as instructors will keep a journal of personal writings which will mirror discoveries and growths.

III: Goals. (1) To gain confidence in the use of communications skills; (2) to explore many languages and understand how they aid and impede communications; (3) to get in touch with ourselves as communicators, to understand our messages to others and their responses; (4) to overcome the barriers to free exchange; and (5) to view our own personal experiences in light of our discoveries.

What is perhaps most noteworthy about this description is its view of communications generally and writing in particular. Usually, "freshmen English" is a skills course: students write themes and teachers correct them. The emphasis is on the mechanics of learning how to write or how to write better. Such a course is, understandably, the sole responsibility of the English instructor. But the tandem approach assumes that while knowing how to write is certainly necessary, this knowledge is not sufficient to produce a competent writer. Awareness and understanding of what and how people feel—about themselves, about others, about "things"—are also essential to good writing. This assumption gives the counselor a chance to come into the classroom and use human relations skills in conjunction with those of the communications instructor, as each focuses on one of the essential elements.

Subjective evaluations indicate that in the tandem classes students experience a sense of integration in their education that speaks to the whole person in ways that isolated courses in isolated disciplines cannot. In addition, the classroom atmosphere is humanized. There is a sense of protection and an environment of permission, both brought about through the interaction of the two instructors. Finally, tandems provide an excellent opportunity for professional growth. The instructor and counselor have an ongoing, semester-long opportunity to observe one another's teaching styles and techniques and the way each relates to students and subject matter.

The approach does have several possible drawbacks. One is the danger that necessary subject matter might be missed. Another is the amount of energy that is spent in putting together and executing a tandem course. And for faculty members, some personal risk is required in such a partnership. Openness, cooperation, understanding, and mutual support are necessities if two people are going to work together successfully.

Another way to begin converting traditional academic subject matter into simultaneous psychological education is to conduct faculty inservice training programs. Because schools have focused almost exclusively on cognitive learning and intellectual functioning, methods for teaching affective subjects are unfamiliar to most faculty members. Values clarification exercises, group dynamics techniques, role playing, games, and simulations are among the possible tools that could be used.

Other Aspects of Implementation. The area surrounding the campus should be assessed to create an inventory of the educational activities conducted by business, industry, and other agencies. Such a list would portray the total potential of the community as a learning resource and permit students and educators to draft off-campus learning designs (Gould, 1973).

Alternate means for providing individualized instruction are the media. Closed-circuit television, films, teaching machines, programmed studies, packaged programs, videotapes, and cassettes add new, flexible opportunities (Weisberger, 1968). The fear that technological instruction will dehumanize the learning process can be transcended by pointing out examples that do not show this outcome. For instance, technology now makes it possible to prepare high-quality materials on campus to meet local needs. And the use of electronic devices to practice skills and of multimedia approaches to disseminate information has added new dimensions to learning (see "Technology in Guidance," 1970, for a more complete description).

Other techniques include team teaching, using students as instructors, and small-group work. One resource, *Practical Approaches to Individualizing Instruction: Contracts and Other Effective Teaching Strategies* (Dunn and Dunn, 1972), presents a variety of effective ways to individualize and personalize instruction. The contract method, which enables students to achieve realistic goals with a minimum of tension and a maximum of self-appreciation, is presented in detail. Brainstorming, circles of knowledge, team learning, role playing, and other techniques for involving students in the learning process are described so that learning will be based on students' abilities, interests, style of learning, and rate of learning and achievement.

A far-reaching suggestion quite compatible with the proposed student development approach has been made by Crookston (1973), who believes the human development component should be given a special place within the institution. By taking on teaching and research functions, it should gain the status of an academic subdivision. But unlike the members of more traditional academic units, the human development educators would offer training in student-centered teaching methods and in basic helping skills to all individual students, faculty, and staff. Included among these skills would be individual and group counseling, problem-solving and the ability to design, complete and evaluate developmental tasks. A collaborative relationship between the department and students would continue through their entire college career, helping students to integrate experiences initiated by others and to take responsibility for changing their lives. The setting could be any on- or off-campus location, including, but not limited to, classrooms, laboratories, and libraries. Rotation of faculty members in and out of the center every four years would create a growing core of teachers who could apply human development concepts in their academic disciplines or professions.

ABILITIES OF THE STUDENT DEVELOPMENT INSTRUCTOR

To carry out the kinds of instruction described here, the educator must know the principles of sound learning theory. A repertoire of strategies such as group discussions, lectures, programmed learning, practical experiences, team projects, and media applications is also required. The educator should be able to create courses for student development and to implement them in the regular curriculum. The ability to teach such subjects as value clarification, decision making, human sexuality, drug and alcohol abuse, and other topics related to the needs and concerns of students is necessary too. Further, he or she should be familiar with the nontraditional learning opportunities and resources available on campus and in the community. And lastly, the professional must be capable of assuming several interrelated roles: teacher, trainer, consultant, and evaluator (Crookston, 1973).

In summary, instruction which advances the growth of each student will have unique characteristics. Learning will be in and out of the classroom and will occur in groups and independently. Flexible time periods for mastery and a variety of methods will allow students to pursue individual objectives. The "teachers" will be academic faculty members, student affairs workers, other adults, and other students. The content will comprise the full range of human concerns and problems and will include relevant learning for living, such as how to make decisions and solve problems, as well as academic subject matter. The student affairs worker will be seen as a partner in an instructional process deliberately planned to educate the whole student, incorporating both personal and intellectual growth.

Chapter 5

꙰꙰꙰꙰꙰꙰꙰꙰

Consultation

Current definitions of consultation have been influenced by the frequent use of consultants in the business world to help develop more effective methods. Lippitt's definition is an example: "A consultation relationship is a voluntary relationship between a professional helper (consultant) and a help-needing system (client) in which the consultant is attempting to give help to the client in the solving of current or potential problems and the relationship is perceived as temporary by both parties. Also, the consultant is an outsider, that is, he is not part of the hierarchical power system in which the client is located" (1959, p. 11).

Because this traditional view deals only with problems and

88

places the consultant outside the system with which he or she works, it has serious limitations in postsecondary education. To overcome these restrictions, Lanning proposes the following: "Consultation is the activity or process in which one person engages with another person, group, or agency in order to identify the needs and/or capabilities of that person, group, or agency and then to plan, initiate, implement, and evaluate action designed to meet and/or develop those needs and/or capabilities" (1974, p. 172).

The number of potential consumers for this type of consultation is clearly much greater than that for a strictly problem-oriented approach. Any unit whose primary goal is to provide excellent educational services is likely to participate in consultation. The student development consultant should try to solve problems, develop the capabilities of others, and influence program direction, but the student, group, or organization must make the ultimate decisions and accept full responsibility for their consequences.

As higher education becomes more complex, it must use its resources in ever more efficient ways. This need leads to extending the services of educational and organizational experts throughout the academic community. And the resulting desire to influence the behavior of as many persons as possible creates a greater interest in consulting (McGehearty, 1968). To be effective in the postsecondary setting, consultation must be based on the assumption that college students are capable of self-direction and that all members of the academic community, be they students, teachers, student affairs workers, or staff members, can benefit and function more effectively as a result of this collaborative activity. As a strategy for change, then, consultation is particularly valuable when student development educators establish colleague relationships with others that produce growth for all concerned. Their joint aim should be serving the developmental needs of more students in more ways.

The consultant can be effective through several means: by providing information and advice; by giving a consultee a chance to ventilate feelings about a difficult case and then return to the problem somewhat refreshed and possibly with a new attitude; by serving as a role model—the consultee can observe the interaction and the manner in which the consultant reacts to the problem; and by reopening communication channels which have been blocked somehow (Zusman, 1972). In a student development context, the consultant should emphasize preventive measures, developing programs and other kinds of intervention aimed at anticipating and meeting the needs of normally functioning individuals before serious problems develop (Conyne and Cochran, 1973).

Fullmer and Bernard (1972) show that student affairs workers need to consult with resource persons—instructors, staff members, or administrators—as well as with individual students, groups, or organizations. The student affairs staff and the faculty should use their skills more effectively to influence the developmental behavior of students on a broader front. For example, the student development consultant could work with teachers to individualize instruction, helping them design learning experiences that are consistent with what is known about students, unify the cognitive and affective aspects of a course, and evaluate the full range of student learning. It must always be remembered, however, that the ultimate targets of consultation are not the resource persons themselves, although their own growth can be advanced, but rather the student population with which they deal.

An example of a useful consultative program was the faculty development workshop *"Understanding the Campus Environment"* offered by the Illinois State University in Normal. Since the campus consists of its ecological structures, its policies, procedures, and programs, its inhabitants, and its psychosocial "climate," it has a large impact on students. Especially important inhabitants are the faculty members, who have direct and significant contacts with learners. This faculty workshop sought to acquaint its participants with the most recent environmental data (particularly regarding the quality of faculty-student relations), to help them explore their own perceptions of the setting, and finally to have them evaluate the data. The workshop sponsors assumed that as faculty became more aware of their deep effect on students, they would do a better job of encouraging students' development.

Consultation

The three-hour workshop, directed toward faculty from diverse academic disciplines, was planned by the director of Measurement and Evaluation Services and staff members from the Counseling Center. They then obtained support from appropriate administrative and academic deans.

A "structure of the environment" scale was used to generate faculty perceptions of what currently "is" in the environment and what "ought to be." An "educational benefits priorities" exercise developed from an Institutional Research Report was also used. In addition, participants completed a four-part evaluation instrument, which included an initial list of goals on a seven-point scale and two post-workshop ratings—one on how well each goal was accomplished, from "completely" to "not at all," and one on how important each goal was to the individual. General comments and suggestions were also solicited.

Another consultation effort is represented by the *Faculty Mini-Workshops* at Eastfield College, Mesquite, Texas, in which faculty groups discuss discrete student populations and their typical actions in class. The student affairs officer provides information concerning stereotypic classroom behavior, facilitates discussion among the faculty members, and helps them to better recognize and understand the dynamics involved.

The way the workshops came about was unusual. The counseling staff felt that they should study the various kinds of behavior that students demonstrate in class and should continually update their information on the characteristics of different student subpopulations. As a start toward these objectives, they generated a list of topics related to the Eastfield student body. Then faculty leaders rated these subjects on their interest value and relevance to expressed faculty concerns. Next, each counselor selected for development one or more of those topics that were personally appealing because of his or her experience or knowledge. To become an "authority" on this subject, the counselor did research, collected data, and organized relevant materials. Finally, the workshop format was chosen as the best means to share this understanding with the faculty. So far, the

91

topics have included: the depressed student, the adult female student, student motivation, student interest patterns, the evening student, the drop-out, and the emotionally distressed student.

The workshops are intended to stimulate faculty discussion. Didactic material is kept to a minimum and used only to introduce the topic and promote faculty interaction. Unlike crisis intervention approaches, the Faculty Mini-Workshops help teachers gain skills in coping with recurring student behavior.

These two examples have shown how the student affairs staff member can work indirectly on student development. But by using direct consultation, one can function more specifically as a facilitator with students. Assuming that assessment has taken place, that the student has been given feedback, and that the consultant and the student have agreed on some goals, the consultant can outline various courses of action the student might take to accomplish them. For example, if the student is lacking in certain social skills, a sequence of activities might be designed to help overcome this awkwardness. Likewise, staff development and inservice education programs can benefit from direct consultation. The personal development of instructors, administrators, and student affairs workers is also essential if the total student development approach is to be realized.

The *Interpersonal Skills Workshop* at Illinois State University in Normal is an example of direct consultation. In this case the consultants are members of the Counseling Center staff and undergraduate paraprofessionals whom the counselors have trained to lead small groups under their supervision. The participants are students or teachers who want to expand their social skills. The workshop is neither remedial nor therapeutic—it is for people who are already functioning adequately but who want to develop more open and honest communication, better identify and express their feelings, and improve their sensitivity to and understanding of others.

The structured laboratory experience includes five weekly two-hour sessions and one weekend six-hour session. One small-group facilitator for each eight participants and one supervisor are required. The workshop also needs a room large enough to accommodate several small groups who must be able to spread out and hold discussions without interference. The activities of both the small groups and the large combined group include short lectures, skill training following demonstration, modeling, supervised practice, and T-group interaction.

As a result of the workshop, participants are expected to learn and practice: (1) being more open and honest with others about themselves; (2) analyzing their own interpersonal style; (3) being more expressive and creative in their responses to others; (4) responding to others in an understanding and helpful manner; and (5) listening to and understanding others' reactions to them. The FIRO-B (Schutz, 1958) is administered and interpreted to stimulate evaluation of their interpersonal style. The Interpersonal Skills Scale (Clack and Conyne, 1973) is also administered before and after the workshop and changes are noted for participants.

Another effort of the Illinois State University, the *Small Group Leadership Workshop: A Professional Development Program,* also illustrates direct consultation with students and faculty. In performing their varied responsibilities, students, staff members, and teachers are often required to lead small groups, committees, student organizations, and the like, although many of them lack any formal training for this role. The nine-hour workshop was designed to give participants a better understanding of small-group theory and skills in applying it. The program is available free to any member of the campus community whose ability to lead groups (or the lack of it) clearly affects the functioning of the university. Seven counselors and one psychology professor collaborated to develop workshop exercises focusing on inclusion, affection, and control in group interaction; discussion guides for group processing; and evaluation materials.

In one weekend workshop accommodating forty students and staff members, participants were randomly assigned to small groups of eight to ten. Two counseling center professionals led each group. Their strategy combined structured small-group experiences and didactic-theoretical components. Each group completed several exercises and discussed the processes involved. Evaluation had several components. First, rank-ordered individual and small-group goals were measured on a seven-point Likert-type scale from "Accomplished none of the goal" to "Accomplished the goal completely." Then discrepancies between the degree to which each individual goal was achieved and the degree to which each should be achieved were measured. Written comments and evaluations were also solicited. And observations were made by group leaders throughout the workshop.

Still another program that incorporates consultation is sponsored and financed by the Department of Counseling and Human Development Services in the College of Education, University of Georgia. The goal of the *Student Development Laboratory* is twofold: first, to facilitate the personal and professional development of graduate students; and second, to provide developmental programming for undergraduates.

The first goal is accomplished through values clarification activities, assertiveness training groups, decision-making groups, personal development groups, and similar experiences, as needed. A contract approach is used in which graduate students identify and plan, with laboratory staff consultation, the specific behavioral objectives which they want to achieve and for which they will receive academic credit. This method is an excellent means for developing their personal responsibility for growth.

After completing a given developmental activity, graduate students are given the opportunity to develop leadership skills in that area by co-leading a training group or other activity for undergraduates. These graduate students prepare an acceptable modular plan outlining the goals, objectives, and processes for the proposed developmental activity. Students ready to participate as co-leaders are individually supervised by laboratory staff members, and regularly scheduled process seminars are held with all co-leaders and supervisors.

The second goal is accomplished with undergraduates and others who have been referred to the Student Development Laboratory by teachers, staff members, academic advisors, and other students. They are assigned to a developmental activity only after completing an assessment interview with a laboratory staff member.

94

Consultation

After completing an inventory and discussing present levels of development, students are informed of the various opportunities they may use to help meet their developmental goals. If the undergraduate chooses a group activity, he or she is placed accordingly. Students may also continue exploration individually with the help of counseling practicum interns who are assigned to the laboratory and supervised by the sponsoring department's faculty.

Operationally speaking, the Student Development Laboratory is a preservice graduate education program that helps to fulfill the training needs of students majoring in Counseling and Human Development Services as well as to meet the personal developmental needs of the student body in general.

THE PROCESS

Assumptions. The following statements about the relationship between human development and consultation should be considered before taking on a consultative role.

(1) The potential for development is inherent in everyone. Each individual can progress in desired directions, especially if his or her growth is assisted by a supportive colleague relationship.

(2) Humans are ultimately responsible for their own actualization. They are all capable of self-direction and consultation assists them in assuming that responsibility.

(3) Consultation can be an aid but not a solution. Since covert events, such as thinking, feeling, and imagining, are perceivable only by the individual experiencing them, they are clearly confined to the realm of self-management. The student development educator is therefore limited to making suggestions or acting as a catalyst—behavior cannot be modified directly, nor should we expect others to feel obliged to follow our proposed directions.

(4) Development calls for new and varied experiences, and it is helpful when others, such as a consultant, can help an individual become exposed to and interpret new experiences in meaningful ways.

Advising Versus Consulting. The steps that are taken in the

95

consultation process depend partly on how the role of the student development educator is defined. Brown (1972) differentiates between consultants and advisors; unlike advisors, consultants are sought as experts by the consultee (instead of being appointed), and they have no final say in the decisions that are made. Thus, consultants are free agents who are not responsible for the action taken, although they may be accountable to those seeking their wisdom. The services of consultants are more likely to be requested in the initial stages of a venture, whereas advisors often enter the picture just before action is to be taken. Brown concludes that the advisor relationship seldom has the ingredients to become a consultant relationship.

On the other hand, Pyron (1974) outlines a method whereby advising can become more like consultation. As a consultant, the student affairs worker would not attend all meetings of the student groups with which he or she worked but rather would offer some training experiences at first to help the members learn how to establish goals, work effectively together, and develop leadership. Then the educator would withdraw from active involvement, yet remain available as a resource whenever the need arose.

Similarly, Yager (1975) describes how the student affairs worker becomes a consultant, one who initiates self-management programs rather than tries to modify behavior directly. As in all counseling, the educator first builds a meaningful relationship with the counselee. But as soon as the student has done enough exploring to decide what kinds of changes are desired, the educator departs from a traditional counseling approach and begins to teach specific methods for gaining self-control and modifying undesired behavior: relaxation, desensitization, thought stopping, assertiveness training, and self-imposed positive or negative reinforcement.

Many contacts between the student affairs staff and students could benefit by having the neutral and short-term characteristics of consultation, although the more prescriptive and lengthy advising process is also useful and necessary. The ideal relationship that Caplan (1970) calls "coordinate interdependence," in which each member gives as well as takes, can exist in either context, as long as the educator does not maintain an "expert" status at the student's expense.

Six Phases. The following steps outlined by Lanning (1974) are particularly relevant to consultation, but they apply generally to advising as well. First, *contact is made.* Parker (1971) presents four ways in which this is likely to occur: a student or campus unit seeks help (in the two hundred colleges surveyed by Pyron in 1974, about 57 percent of the consultative relationships were initiated in this traditional manner); after an assessment is made, help is offered, often in a counseling relationship (nearly 48 percent of the consultations began like this); an individual or group is required to accept help and make some change as a condition of continued affiliation with the organization (about 23 percent); or consultation is a routine function in a continuing effort to develop an individual, group, or organization (about 34 percent of the relationships were of this kind).

Lanning feels that an extensive public relations program to make the whole campus community aware of the consultation function will generate many contacts. Conversely, Conyne and Cochran (1973) believe it is more appropriate to develop well-specified, attainable goals in a few carefully selected areas than to try to effect massive changes throughout the organization. Consultations with faculty members may begin when a professor inquires about a student or when an administrator or teacher invites a student affairs person to work with the faculty of a school or college. Effective consultation on an initially limited basis which is particularly constructive should result in increasing acceptance of the performance of this function by the student affairs worker.

Second, *the consultant enters the relationship.* Before beginning, the consultant must be clear about goals, the limits of his or her ability, and the limits of consultation itself. When one enters an organizational unit, one needs to understand its hierarchy of authority. The consultant can expect to implement a plan successfully only up to the authority level of the person with whom the initial agreement was made.

Third, *needs are identified.* If the consultee is a student, this assessment takes the forms described in Chapter Three. If the consultant is working with an academic unit or the administration, discussions are held with individual members of the group or the unit as a whole. In some cases, research may be designed to assess needs. The outcome of this phase—an informal, verbal one for the student, a more formal appraisal otherwise—should be a report along with the consultant's recommendations. At this point the consultant's job may be over if the individual or group decides to proceed on its own.

Fourth, *implementation begins*. If his or her services are still desired, the student development educator provides a detailed plan for carrying out the proposed recommendations. As part of this plan, the consultant may even assume the role of trainer in a pilot project.

Fifth, *an evaluation is made*. The assessment design should be part of the plan for implementation, and evaluation should occur automatically at least once, at the end of the procedure, and maybe at several intermediate points as well.

Finally, *the relationship is terminated*. In Lanning's model, the inside consultant must officially withdraw once the ongoing activity is initiated. It is important that the student or group be able to follow through with the program without the working assistance of the consultant.

Another, more specific consultation process is presented by Conyne and Cochran (1973), who describe how a university counseling center assisted students' career development. Before planning and implementing an intervention, the center articulated its philosophy of counseling and decided it could help students examine their employment interests and choices. Next, the staff members identified the "target." Since the literature indicates clearly that the faculty has a powerful effect on the student's choice of a career, the counselors selected three academic fields—history, industrial technology, and art—in which to concentrate their efforts. Working with the chairperson and five selected faculty members in each department, one of the consultants compiled a list of activities related to career development that teachers might perform. Each faculty member ranked the activities twice: first in order of actual performance and second in order of ideal importance.

Consultation

The consultant and the chairperson examined the discrepancies between the actual and ideal rankings, particularly those concerning academic advisement. Then, after several meetings with all the faculty members, the counselor drew up a proposal suggesting that academic advising should relate educational goals to future career goals; faculty members should consistently seek consultations with the placement and counseling center; and academic advising should not continue or expand unless evaluation proves its effectiveness. Assessments of this consultation process indicated that many of the faculty members became more positive about undertaking career-related activities with students.

CONSULTANT ACTIVITIES

The survey by Pyron (1974), referred to earlier, indicated that extracurricular matters are frequently the subject of consultation. Table 2 shows how often particular activities were performed by student personnel workers.

TABLE 2. Consultant Activities of Student Personnel Workers

	Mean*
Help groups accomplish goals	6.2
Diagnose student conflict	6.1
Assist in long-range planning	5,6
Improve group decision making	5.7
Perform student-life research	5.3
Help groups become cohesive	5.5
Build student leadership skills	5.0
Use behavioral contracts	5.2
Train individuals as paraprofessionals	4.9
Improve groups' interpersonal relations	4.7
Train groups in goal setting	4.6
Train groups in problem solving	4.7
Help faculty understand student problems	4.6
Help faculty understand student development	4.3
Observe the process of group meetings	3.3
Work with academic department organizational problems	2.2
Conduct workshop for faculty	1.9

*Each item was rated on a scale from 1, "Never," to 7, "Regular Practice."
Source: Pyron, 1974, p. 266.

From this study it appears obvious that although student affairs people regularly consult with students, they infrequently consult with faculty members. Since faculty involvement is essential to the student development program, it becomes important that student affairs members seek to strengthen their consultative relationships with all segments of the academic community.

Using performance contracts to achieve specific ends is an innovative method of direct consultation (Ehrle, 1970). The parties to this formal agreement define what kinds of student behavior they seek, and then the student, in collaboration with the student affairs worker, sets up appropriate activities. The student as consumer always has the final word.

Modeling is another form of consultation. The student affairs worker can be an excellent live model by demonstrating a desired behavior and arranging optimum environmental conditions in which the client can do the same. As a model of how to manage relationships, the educator can help a student acquire new social skills that can be applied outside the consultation setting. Symbolic models can also be used to initiate the desired behavior. First, the educator presents some written material about the skill to be learned. Then the student watches or listens to an audiotape, videotape, or film in which individuals illustrate the behavior desired. Finally, the student experiments with the new behavior under observation (Nye, 1973).

Challenge Activities at Auburn. Learning to model community living skills was an important goal of a nontraditional program conducted by the Auburn University Department of Housing. Staff members felt that resident assistants in the dorms should have the ability to promote student development by modeling responsible and responsive behavior and by encouraging residents to take initiative, become involved, and direct their own growth. The program philosophy was similar to Powell's contention that "inservice education should provide the resident assistant with an increasing understanding of his own development, his strengths and weaknesses, his own characteristics; and it should give him increasingly confident means by which he can use the internal understanding of himself to enhance growth in others" (1974, p. 204).

Consultation

The staff of the Men's Housing Department chose an unfamiliar environment—the wilderness—in which to integrate techniques developed by Outward Bound, Inc., and the Ranger and Special Forces units of the United States Army. Their purpose was to stimulate both personal development and understanding of group processes. Specifically, the individual objectives were four—self-esteem, self-awareness, self-assertion, and acceptance of others. These aims were expressed as follows: resident assistants should increase their acceptance of both personal strengths and weaknesses and should have a greater sense of personal worth. Resident assistants should show they have engaged in self-examination and feel in touch with themselves. Awareness of emotions, abilities, potentials, and limitations should increase. There should be a demonstrated increase in willingness to assume leadership and responsibility, as well as new confidence in their abilities to tackle a realistic challenge. Toward others increased tolerance and compassion should be shown, regardless of their weaknesses or strengths. Lastly, more competence in building strong human relationships and acceptance of the responsibility for doing so should be acknowledged.

In order to accomplish these objectives, the instructors *impelled* resident assistants into a variety of challenging activities that would demand more of them than they would demand of themselves. Among these were rock climbing, rappelling, learning survival skills, orienteering, physical training, and readings (on coping with adversity, meeting challenge, personal growth). The training format incorporated the following elements:

(1) *Small group process.* A group identity is easily achieved by striving and working together with the activities at hand. Superordinate goals bring diverse groups together.

(2) *Responsibility.* Instructors demonstrate activities and ensure safety, but learning comes through the performance or nonperformance of the resident assistant.

(3) *Immediate application of skills.* Only the skill or knowledge needed to carry out an activity is taught—just before it is applied.

(4) *Graduated challenges.* Increasingly difficult tasks estab-

101

lish a pattern of success and require renewed effort to gain feelings of accomplishment.

(5) *Simplified environment*. This setting is an effective teacher, dispensing immediate and appropriate consequences for action or inaction: no shelter—gets wet; builds fire—is warm. However, intervention may be required if the "lesson" is potentially dangerous to the welfare of the group or the individual (an improperly tied knot may cause a serious injury).

(6) *Day and night programming*. Continuous training provides an intensive experience in confronting self and others on more than superficial levels. Unremitting challenge and contrasts of hot/cold, dry/wet, tired/rested, excited/bored, together/alone help sharpen perceptions.

(7) *A performance-centered guidance approach*. Assuming that people feel better after they do better, the program emphasizes doing first and exploring feelings about self and others afterward.

During the six-day session, the male resident assistants had to trade watching for doing, talking for acting, indifference for commitment. They were put in predicaments requiring them to take initiative, rely on others for their own safety, and care for and help others. In practically every instance, decision making was left to the individual and to team members. For example, from the very start, teams had to determine what and how much they would eat and how they would prepare it. The instructors intervened infrequently and only to ensure the safety of the individuals.

Self-reports submitted by the resident assistants and verbal evaluations made by the instructors suggested that many of the objectives had been achieved. Most participants said they gained a better understanding of themselves, their strengths, weaknesses, potentials, and coping behaviors. Many indicated that for the first time they really understood the meaning of being a contributing group member and the processes necessary for effective group functioning.

Academic Consultation Service (ACS). Quite different activities are undertaken by the consultants at Howard University, Washington, D.C., where they work with older students who are returning to college and students who have one or more of the following learning difficulties: poor study habits, poor planning, procrastination, indecisiveness, or the inability to establish goals. The faculty and staff try to give students visible support, as well as furnish assistance that will make their first year of college reentry or reinstatement a little less stressful and more satisfying. In addition to providing reassurance, the consultants make sure the students know what is expected of them and what resources are available.

The heart of this behavioral management program is the cooperative relationship between the student and the consulting staff. The student's role is to take responsibility for change, because the opportunities offered by this program extend only as far as the student's interests and commitment. The other two members of the team are the advisor and the counselor. The advisor is the crucial link between the student's classroom performance and any manifest change in academic progress. The student, with aid from the advisor, plans class schedules and course sequences that will reduce the difficulties of readjustment. The counselor's role is to help the student by identifying barriers to academic success and recommending "assist units" appropriate to the student's needs and goals. Involvement in the program is voluntary, but contractual. Once the student makes a commitment, he or she is expected to make maximum use of the services. The advisor and the counselor help the student meet the terms of the agreement.

The assist units are short workshops lasting one or two days or topical one-hour sessions each week for as many as eight weeks. The content of the study skills unit is self-evident—learning to organize assignments, prepare for exams, take class notes, use resources, and the like. The test anxiety program uses systematic desensitization procedures to help students who have a history of panic and mental blockage during tests. Applying the principle of self-reinforcement, the motivation/assertiveness training is for students who seem to be easily frustrated and unable to set goals, show poor self-discipline, and tend to be academically nonassertive. The workshop on vocational/educational decision making, which helps students choose a major and make tentative employment plans, includes assessment and gives some attention to decision making itself. The purpose of the personal adjustment group is to assist individuals whose discomfort and anxiety result from stressful relationships, family problems, and poor self-concept.

Students as Consultants. Another type of consultant activity is the basis of the Peer Academic Advising Program at the University of Georgia in Athens. The program was initiated by the Housing Office, which proposed to the College of Arts and Sciences that the roles of resident assistant and academic advisor be combined. The College agreed, and faculty and staff members began interviewing and selecting students to become peer advisors. In the last phase of their 220-hour training, the students observed faculty advising and practiced advising with faculty supervision.

These paraprofessionals live on the same floor as their advisees, the freshmen residents, and throughout the year they work together. The staff-student ratio of 1:32 makes both individual and group contact manageable and effective. The objectives of the advisors are: (1) to provide information on university requirements and procedures and do academic advising; (2) to help the freshmen formulate objectives congruent with their interests and skills; (3) to conduct a study skills workshop; and (4) to offer programs on choosing an academic major and planning a career. A general goal is to build a community atmosphere in their living unit that is conducive to academic success and personal development.

Before the peer advising begins, each freshmen takes the SAT, the university's English and math placement tests, and the Brown and Holtzman Survey of Study Habits and Attitudes. In addition, all advisees complete the Omnibus Personality Inventory while others fill out the Student Developmental Task Inventory on an individualized consultation basis. Using this assessment information, each peer advisor consults with his or her advisees at least twice each quarter on academic and developmental subjects. One session includes preparing a class schedule for the following quarter. The advisor uses the SSHA results to help the freshmen acquire the study skills they need—how to manage their time, take notes, prepare for tests, and take exams.

The peer advisor is also expected to help students design

104

developmental goals and strategies. In fulfilling this task, the advisor can solicit the aid of professionals on the campus. These "student development" consultants provide guidance and conduct seminars on such topics as career development, self-discovery, sexual identity, and exploring the university. In subsequent consulting sessions, the advisor helps the freshmen determine their achievement and make further plans.

The program is evaluated in three ways. The students evaluate the whole effort and, with the assistance of their advisor, their individual attainment. The peer advisors also judge the program as well as their own performance. And finally, both the professional and paraprofessional staff examine their success against criteria established at the beginning of the program.

The potential of students as consultants for enhancing student development has barely been tapped so far. With the importance of training peers as student development staff members in mind, the ACPA monograph *Student Paraprofessionals: A Working Model for Higher Education* (Delworth and others, 1974) and the WICHE publication *Training Manual for Paraprofessional and Allied Professional Programs* (Delworth and Aulepp, 1976) are particularly relevant.

A Consultation Agency. By becoming aware of current models, practitioners will be able to design programs of their own. One example which appears particularly worthwhile because of its integrated concept is the Center for Institutional Self-Renewal proposed by Parker (1971). Faculty from academic departments and from student affairs offices would study the university's efforts to meet the needs of its students and simultaneously offer professional consultation on educational programs to various segments of the institution. The staff members would include logocentrists, practicentrists, and democentrists. Logocentrists are behavioral scientists whose primary task is doing research on the processes of higher education, particularly on what happens to students at college. Armed with useful theories of student development and their research results, these faculty members would build models of individual and organizational change. Practicentrists are skilled at improving the

105

functioning of individuals, small groups, and organizations. They would be able to consult with groups, including academic departments, to apply their colleagues' models in designing educational experiences. The key to change would be a developmental contract which details mutually acceptable goals. The democentrists interpret the accumulating knowledge to the educational community. The focus of such a research, consultation, and dissemination unit is on student learning, wherever and however it occurs.

KNOWLEDGE AND SKILLS OF THE CONSULTANT

In assuming the consultant role, the student affairs professional will need to practice a number of skills. Probably the first requirement is constructing an effective consulting relationship. Lauver (1974) points out that simply following steps and working "solutions" does not guarantee this result. The consultant's attitude is important, for he or she must demonstrate the belief that the consultee has the right to decide whether or not to accept help and help with what. Consultative success is derived directly from the willingness of both parties to be involved in each step. A potential hazard is becoming caught up with the *what* (the desired changes or goals) and neglecting the *how* (the sequence of activities initiated and carried on by the consultant that establish the relationship). If the consultant pays attention to building and strengthening their relationship, the goal attainment of all will be enhanced.

An important component of this relationship is the ability to communicate personal or professional values. Since the capacity to influence the consultee results partly from possessing values and actions desired by this person, the consultant as model must definitely be aware of his or her beliefs. In fact, one's effectiveness may even depend on being able to state these feelings and attitudes explicitly.

To work effectively with groups, the student affairs worker should know how to help them set goals, develop leadership and power, and make decisions. Effective observation techniques should also be acquired. Similar skills are needed for fostering the individual development of leadership qualities, good human relations, and

106

awareness of others. To develop these abilities one must first be aware of oneself as a social being because one is sure to encounter opposing language barriers and differences in goals that require perceptive handling.

If student affairs workers are to provide help with long- and short-range planning, diagnosing student conflict, and decision making, they must develop research and evaluation skills. By gathering data on issues related to students and their environment and making it available for decision making, they can give valuable assistance. Systematic application of research on how attitudes, perceptions, and feelings develop and change would likewise help the consultant (Kramer, 1972).

If student affairs workers are to respond to the full array of individual and social needs and to the full range of people now attending college, they must move toward and improve on intervention modes such as consultation. Student affairs workers acting as consultants must proceed in careful planned ways, for their overall goal is to promote self-help: a direct result of successful consultation efforts will be an increasingly greater awareness of the value of the consultation process by others within the campus community. As this awareness grows, so will the opportunities for increased involvement of student affairs practitioners as key participants in the educational process.

Chapter 6

❧❧❧❧❧❧❧❧

Environmental Management

For many student affairs workers, *management* smacks of manipulation and coldness, the opposites of what they are looking for when they entered a field characterized by helping relationships. The reasons for their antipathy are understandable. Since most have been educated as counselors, they know little about techniques for altering the academic environment. And those who reject behavior modification as an undesirable strategy often suggest that students should be the ones to change their surroundings. These professionals rarely see themselves as having the necessary leverage for action.

These views, however, are narrow and potentially stifling.

Environmental Management

The student's world—milieu—comprises the physical environment, the human community, the academic curriculum, and many other tangibles and intangibles. Managing this world does not mean controlling it. It means a positive, collaborative effort by all community members, students, student affairs workers, teachers, and administrators, to organize their resources so that students get the most out of their college experience. Student development educators should apply whatever scientific methods they possess to foster full personal growth and institutional change. The position taken by Banks and Martens (1973) that helping professionals must function as agents of social change, seeking to improve any conditions that create problems for individuals, appears sound.

"Objective" observers often question whether anyone has the right and the power to define the behavior and attitudes of those living in an environment, even when the definitions are drawn from the mainstream of American cultural values and standards. Ethical concerns about experimental manipulations of people who are unaware of what is being done are valid, but a managed milieu need not imply a naive student clientele. If everyone in the campus community cooperates to clarify their goals and make plans, and if students guide their own participation, unethical practices should not result.

THEORETICAL CONSIDERATIONS

Normal maturation brings changes irrespective of the environment, but growth is unlikely to proceed in a positive direction if damaging influences are everpresent. It is not surprising, therefore, to find that research documents the effect of the physical environment on student development. Astin (1968) and Pace (1967) suggest that students attending small colleges tend to perceive them as being more friendly, cohesive, group-oriented, and less competitive than the larger institutions seem to their peers. Chickering (1969) also supports the thesis that college size has an impact on the effectiveness of the educational process for some students. In large universities, the sheer numbers, the proliferation of courses, the limited participation in extra-academic activities, and numerous other conditions sharply limit the possibilities for developing relationships outside small, informal friendship groups formed after chance encounters. When enrollment is small, when resources are limited; when students, faculty and administration alike are making do with less than ideal or adequate facilities; when staff members serve in several capacities and work with students in varying contexts; and when student resources are needed, a high level of unity usually exists. A strong identification with the institution develops, and the total college community becomes an effective culture for its members.

Newcomb (1962) and Chickering (1969) discuss how living arrangements can foster or inhibit exchange between individuals, since the evidence for the principle that propinquity breeds close interpersonal relationships is unequivocal. Chickering hypothesizes that interior and exterior architecture and the location of units in relation to each other affect the range and intensity of associations which occur. Environments select and shape the behavior of people who inhabit them, according to Barker's behavior setting theory (Walsh, 1975). The number of inhabitants is an especially important variable. For example, people in undermanned situations seem to be busier, more vigorous, more versatile, and more involved, and consequently they seem to be personally more productive and satisfied than those in a fully staffed milieu.

According to the subculture concept (Walsh, 1975), consistent person-environment relationships tend to stimulate satisfying human associations as well as maintain and reinforce certain attitudes and behavior. Similarly, Holland's research (1973) indicates that congruent interactions between the individual and the milieu are associated with personal and vocational stability and satisfaction. Stern (1970) believes that a relatively congruent person-environment relationship (combination of "needs" and "press") produces a sense of fulfillment, while a relatively dissonant relationship (unstable needs-press combination) produces stress.

But other research has not always supported these hypotheses. Pervin (1968b), for instance, suggests that students may tend to be more satisfied and productive in a college where their self-perceptions do not completely fit their views of the environment. A somewhat imperfect match, in effect, presents more opportunities for change. And Feldman and Newcomb (1969, p. 332) observe that, initially, too great a divergence between student and college may elicit resistance, whereas too little might mean no impetus for growth. College is likely to have the greatest impact on students who experience a continuing series of not too threatening discontinuities.

Clearly, then, the environment has a variety of effects on individual development. Probably not all incongruencies should be eliminated, even if they could be; nevertheless, if student development educators do nothing to manage campus resources, learning is left to chance and the results may be counterproductive.

THE DEVELOPMENTAL MILIEU

The ideal environment for student development is characterized by certain principles. First, the various elements in it must serve common institutional goals. When students participate in activities that share an integrated purpose, the college moves closer to meeting this criterion. There must be a common denominator in the functioning of all staff members, namely, the affirmation of student development as the goal of postsecondary education. Efforts to promote a fertile environment will not produce maximum growth if faculty or others are hostile to the goal and if they go about their teaching isolated from it (Pervin, 1968a). Yet, as previously mentioned, a fragmented campus is the rule, not the exception. The fact that the college's values and aims are rarely made explicit may be both a symptom and part of the problem.

Second, there must be a purposeful relationship between formal learning and the student's growth outside the classroom. What is needed is the integration of the scholar and the social being, of the learning and the whole person. Academic tasks, in effect, should be determined by the psychological readiness of the student to pursue them and by the answers to two questions: Do they support the student's maturation? And will they help develop the abilities needed to deal effectively with life's realities?

111

Much of a student's success or failure in college can be attributed to the way time outside class is used. If a student lives in an environment that encourages and rewards academic inquiry, academic success is more likely. But if one spends most of the time in a purely social milieu, the opportunity to realize one's full academic potential will be lessened.

The third principle of a developmental environment is that a reasonable degree of compatibility between an individual and the college is necessary to promote maximum growth. Research has been cited earlier on this principle, and further support is provided by Heisler (1961), who stated that a "dynamic equilibrium" exists between the needs and capacities of the student and the levels of stress and stimulation in the environment. When these levels are far above one's "readiness" to cope, one tends to withdraw and opportunities to grow are lost. But when too little stimulation is available, the student's development is slowed because of a lack of challenges and opportunities. Like Pervin, Sanford (1966) recommends that the environment disturb the person's equilibrium so that new learning will result. At the same time, a developmental community must be able to assess with great accuracy the ability of the individual to withstand stress and make use of up-ending influences. Because it is difficult to be accurate about such tolerance, it is necessary to have supportive resources available to sustain persons through crises.

Fourth, there must be a true relationship between what occurs on the campus and what happens in the "real world." The plea for educational relevance by students should not fall on deaf ears. Too often in the past, college students experienced a world surrounded by ivy walls that tended to protect them from what was going on elsewhere. But educational isolationalism is a luxury students can ill afford today. Since "real" people must function in the "real" world, the more integrated the learning community with the larger community, the better. Crookston (1973) describes the developmental milieu in terms of a symbiotic or mutually growth-producing relationship between the individual and society. As the individual contributes to the enrichment of society, so the society is able in return to enrich the individual. Establishment of such symbiotic environments would help students learn the importance of

112

interdependence in their lives, a characteristic essential to survival in the world of tomorrow. By offering students opportunities to develop the abilities required to be successful and productive citizens, higher education is responding to a major social need. It is unlikely that such learning can come from the classroom alone. Practice in situations where "real" consequences follow "real" actions helps to enhance the value of developmental learning. One application of this approach created by Crookston (1974) was the "Intentional Democratic Community," a living environment planned to stimulate the growth of the participants as well as the community they created.

The fifth and perhaps the single most important principle is that an effective milieu responds to the developmental needs of its inhabitants. Grant (1974) states that five environmental elements are essential to support the growth of a human being in a natural way. *Stimulation* is the first requirement. Just to exist, as well as to function well, people need an adequate amount and variety of stimuli, whatever their content. At the same time, they need *security* or protection from unwanted or undesirable stimuli. This is often identified as the need for privacy. Another requirement, particularly in the academic environment, is *order*. An orderly setting tends to support intellectual activity, while a confusing milieu inhibits such behavior and invites frustration. Yet a totally or overly ordered environment can stifle creativity and innovation, so humans should have *freedom* to create their own environment. And finally, each person needs to have dominion over his or her personal property, "life space," and functioning within that space. When individuals are allowed to stake out a piece of the environment for themselves, over which they have maximum control, they can determine the level of security, stimulation, order, and freedom that they want around them. This, in essence, allows them to develop *territoriality*.

FUNCTIONAL EXAMPLES OF MILIEU MANAGEMENT

The five principles of milieu management are reflected in the following examples.

EDGE Program. The Educational Development Group Enrichment Program at Bowling Green State University attempted to create an active strategy to help students structure their living environment within the academic community. Its objectives were to increase students' academic achievement, accelerate their maturation, help them choose a career, and ease their transition to college. The participants in this one-year pilot program were freshmen and sophomore men living in the residence halls. The staff members included one full-time professional hall director, one undergraduate resident advisor, three psychologists working part-time as consultant advisors, and one professor from the political science department, who was a part-time resource person for the residents.

The EDGE program was initiated by the Office of Residence Programs with the advice and assistance of members of the Counseling Center and a student affairs consultant from another institution. Although students did not play a critical role in originating the program, its implementation was directed entirely by a joint student-staff committee. At these meetings progress was charted, new workshops and interest areas were planned, and changes were made. For all practical purposes, after the initial adjustment period of approximately five weeks, the EDGE students were responsible for determining the direction of the program with the advice of the professional staff. The final phase of the program comprised a complete review of the program by the students and the staff, a goal-free evaluation, and a new goal-setting program.

The behavioral objectives were the following:

(1) Of the EDGE freshmen, 80 percent or more will have a GPA after the first quarter at least half a point higher than their highest predicted ACT college gradepoint.

(2) Of the EDGE sophomores, 80 percent will show an increase of .3 of a point or more over (1) their GPA of the previous spring quarter and (2) their overall GPA.

(3) The mean GPA of all the EDGE students will be at least half a point higher than the average GPA of the freshmen and sophomore class at BGSU at the end of each quarter.

(4) EDGE students will show a higher level of social and maturational growth, as measured by the Omnibus Personality Inventory, than the general college population standard set by the OPI at the end of the academic year.

114

(5) EDGE freshmen will exhibit, as observed by the resident assistants and the hall director, fewer adjustment difficulties in adapting to college life.

(6) Seventy percent of the EDGE students will report on the College and University Environment Assessment Scale greater satisfaction with their residence hall experience than a randomly selected group of students from the same residence hall and a group from one other randomly chosen men's residence hall.

(7) Students participating in the career and life planning programs as part of the EDGE experience will exhibit less career anxiety, be more confident in their selection of a major course of study, and develop a better understanding of their personal needs and values, as reported in individual counseling interviews at the beginning and end of the academic year.

The program was designed to meet a variety of student needs through regular course instruction, developmental workshops, individual counseling, roommate matching, a controlled study environment, and special diagnostic testing. Students were allowed to choose from a number of options those growth experiences they felt they needed. This self-selection process is based on the principle that the individual provided with the necessary information can best determine his or her own requirements.

Specifically, each student was matched with a roommate from a similar academic area, but the pair was located near students with different majors. All the students in the living unit planned programs on subjects of special interest to them, using such aids as speakers and films. The political science faculty member regularly visited the unit to talk to individuals, help them plan field trips, and lead discussions on current topics. To improve their study habits, a special three-credit course, called Optimum Learning and Academic Success, was given only for them in the residence hall. In addition, a study environment was provided in the hall and nightly quiet hours were observed. On the developmental front, students were offered a series of workshops on such topics as human potential growth, career and life planning, assertiveness training, and biofeedback training.

A number of diagnostic and evaluative measures were used. The Omnibus Personality Inventory, as noted in the objectives, measured personal development. The Strong-Campbell Interest Inventory and the Work Values Inventory were used to determine changes in career orientation and to assist career counseling. The Brown-Holtzman Survey of Study Habits and Attitudes assessed the students' study orientation and measured improvement. The Myers-Briggs Type Indicator was used as a predicator of possible friendship patterns in the living unit and as a form of control over the self-selection by participants. The American College Testing scores and the students' grades determined academic progress. The College and University Environmental Scale (CUE II) was used to determine the students' perception of their living environment.

Each week the joint student-staff committee reviewed progress, and at the end of the quarter (ten weeks) they prepared a written evaluation. The results were discussed with the students and the student affairs administrators throughout the campus. Their reactions and recommendations were compiled and discussed in a meeting of all the EDGE students. In addition, each student had an opportunity to give a "goal-free" assessment during an interview at the beginning and end of each quarter. Finally, the results of the year's effort were summarized and discussed with the students in a group meeting so that plans could be made for the future. Specific outcome data were not available as this book went to press, but they can be obtained by writing to the program directors (see Appendix).

Auburn Residential Program. Although the five environmental elements outlined by Grant are important, they have seldom been consciously and consistently engineered into formal education programs. Auburn University is one institution that has done so, however, by giving students control over many aspects of their milieu. For example, students are free to paint and decorate their rooms to suit their individual tastes—they may paint furniture, paper, or panel walls, plaster ceilings, construct partitions, replace light fixtures, and construct new furniture. They may also bring in stereos, refrigerators, hot plates, and other appliances. The university provides mutual support in the form of two gallons of free paint.

This freedom also extends to hallways, stairwells, and activity rooms, which are considered group territory. The floor unit has five gallons of free paint and its "floor funds" at its discretion. And each fall a contest is held to determine the best decorated rooms and hallways. A total of $600 in prize money is awarded to winners for their creativity, execution of design, and the overall decorating impact of their work. The security element is available in private rooms, which compose about half those available. Understandably, single rooms are highly valued by students because they appear to give students the best way to create their own environment and consequently maintain desirable levels of stimulation, security, freedom, and order.

Group stimulation and order are provided in special "zones." A recreation area comprises a pool room, an electronic game room, a ping pong room with kitchenette, and two color-TV lounges. Since the area is relatively isolated from the students' rooms, a broad range of stimuli can be provided: a variety of odors, sounds, and visual phenomena are always present in varying intensities. Other stimulation zones include a comprehensive health club, an auto mechanics club, and an outdoor recreation program. Order is expected to prevail in the study lounge, where study partners (undergraduate scholars) provide free tutorial assistance in seven subjects four days each week. The environment is highly structured, orderly, and organized around specific activities.

In addition to providing these five basics, the staff wanted to develop a comprehensive group system. One strategy they use is to match roommates with similar academic interests and complementary personality types, as determined by the Myers-Briggs Type Indicator (Myers and Briggs, 1962). They are considered complementary when they have the "dominant process" in common: sensors are paired with sensors, intuitives with intuitives. But the "auxiliary function" varies with each pair in order to encourage growth within the relationship. Through modeling, each individual should help the other to develop the uncharacteristic behavior.

This concept of complementariness is carried further to the floor units, which are assigned on the basis of commonality of dominant process. So one unit may be composed of sensors, another

117

of feeling types. The staff believes these similarities promote a sense of group unity and cohesion and help the students meet their needs for stimulation, security, freedom, and order.

The size and governance of the floor units also support these concepts. The units range in size from nine to thirty students. Since the ideal group size appears to be from eight to twenty members, the staff and students have partitioned certain floors. In the smaller groups, students have more opportunities to be involved in activities and to influence decisions. And smallness helps them function without any student government structure and with a minimum of imposed rules and regulations. Under the peer governance system, groups may elect to establish their own standards, but they don't have to. Control is vested in membership, and each unit decides, for example, how it will use its floor funds, whether or not pets will be permitted to live in the unit, what procedures will be used for recruiting new members, and how the group's territory will be maintained.

Each living unit has an upperclassman resident advisor who functions as a role model, catalyst, consultant, confrontation agent, and quasi-counselor. He does not attempt to control behavior or make decisions, but rather helps to stimulate problem solving by keeping communication open. Resident advisors are generally selected from among men nominated by the students in their units.

In many dorms on other campuses, the staff continues to be confronted with problems of student dissatisfaction, misconduct, excessive damages, and low retention. Such difficulties usually arise from such environmental factors as inadequately designed facilities, unsystematic and arbitrary grouping procedures, and unnecessary rules and regulations. But at Auburn, students develop and exhibit intense pride in their living units. By committing considerable time, effort, and their own financial resources to the personalization of their rooms and hallways, students develop possessive and protective attitudes toward their habitats. Not only do they refrain from destroying what they create, they defend their territory against intruders with malicious intent. Hence, damages are minimal, and increased student satisfaction leads to increased retention. High retention is essential in an effective group system because returning upperclass residents help stabilize the living unit by ensuring that group standards are clarified and transmitted to new members.

Project Greek. The chapter development project at Iowa State University in Ames provides nearly three thousand fraternity and sorority residents with a wide range of programs that support their total educational experience. Since what happens to a student during the first year has a significant impact on his or her overall satisfaction and future development, the project tries to change many of the traditional aspects of the pledge programs for new members. Two main goals of the program are to help students make a positive transition to the university and to develop and manage an educational community that is controlled by the expressed needs of the affiliated residents. The Greek Affairs staff of the Office of Student Life coordinates the program, with the administrative help of undergraduate practicum students, active chapter presidents, and faculty alumni/ae advisors. Except for two organizational development retreats, activities are held on campus. The program is completed and the post-test administered by the beginning of spring quarter each year.

The program began after a survey of fourteen hundred resident Greek students indicated a need for some developmental activities and for better management and pledge programs. The project designers sought to enhance the feeling of belonging and camaraderie that are often cited as the most favorable aspects of fraternities and sororities. For this purpose they established a series of "laboratory" experiences, called units, which enable the participants to experiment with change at a time when they are establishing lifelong patterns. The units are flexible so that individual chapters can adapt them to suit their needs.

Unit 1: The whole house—new pledges, alums, and chapter members—participates in a one-evening orientation session held at the close of the recruitment period. Get-acquainted exercises are used to help everyone feel more open and comfortable. Then the "official business" gets under way. The officers provide information on the expectations and rules that apply to all members and on the general operation of the chapter. The recently completed recruitment process is evaluated with a special instrument designed to give the chapters experience in using formal assessment techniques. Members also complete the Iowa State University Greek Profile, which measures their attitudes on five general topics. The results are used to determine what kinds of changes and programs are desirable. To prevent disputes about the membership development (pledge) program, each member has a voice in determining what the chapter expects of the pledges before they can qualify for initiation. Finally, the new affiliates learn about the importance of keeping a written journal describing their pledging experiences and about the big brother/big sister program.

Unit 2: The second program gives pledges a deeper orientation. Members describe the national and local heritage of the sorority or fraternity; place the membership experience in a perspective that allows new members to see how it will affect their development; expose typical chapter problems before they become burning issues. The new affiliates also get some information on campus resources and some training in parliamentary procedure. All the participants suggest topics that the membership development chairperson (pledge trainer) might use in structuring special meetings or programs for new members. Overall, the purpose of Unit 2 meetings is to see that new members are incorporated in the committee or task-force structure and that they attend two or three regular meetings a month. In so doing, the chapter hopes to develop capable and active members rather than pledges who generally need a full term to catch on to things before they either become productive or lose interest.

Unit 3: The aim of this one-day or overnight chapter retreat is organizational development. The Greek Affairs staff helps the chapter develop a comprehensive structure for chapter programming, using a "management by objectives" approach. Chapter committees are changed to task forces, and members learn about creative problem solving.

Unit 4: Since some chapters maintain separate pledge-class structures and do not involve their new affiliates in most chapter meetings, the project provides this special unit to give their pledge trainers suggestions on programs.

Unit 5: Fraternities and sororities represent an ideal labora-

120

tory setting for the development of leadership potential because their members have so much autonomy in directing chapter operations. Therefore, new affiliates participate in a leadership education program in which they learn about leadership styles that promote involvement and increased productivity and creativity. They also find out how people tend to act and react in organizations, how power and affiliation work together; they learn that building a working team is essential and that people support what they help create. As they gain experience in working in small groups, the pledges learn to apply their knowledge to the leadership of the fraternity or sorority chapter.

Unit 6: To help the chapters make their pre-initiation week as meaningful as possible, the staff suggests several developmental activities. The chapter can, for instance, undertake a service project, which tends to promote unity among the members. The university Volunteer Center can assist them. Another option is a two-hour lab experience, led by the Greek Affairs advisors, which utilizes music and structured group experiences to explore the meaning of friendship and fraternal membership—just pre-initiates (neophytes) or the entire chapter can participate. The pre-initiates should have a special time to review and share the most important aspects of their Greek experiences so far; beforehand, they should have completed their journals. And each chapter should offer special programs or ceremonies that will prepare the pre-initiates for the activation ceremony.

Unit 7: A chapter retreat scheduled for late winter quarter is the final element of Project Greek. Here, the members review the management by objectives format that was instituted in the fall as they evaluate the progress of the individual task forces. And after examining the information generated by the chapter recruitment evaluation instrument that was administered in the fall, they finish their rush plans. The members also complete the Greek Profile to determine whether any attitudes have changed since the beginning of the year.

A Cross-Cultural Community. As the group-development aspect of the Auburn University model shows, humans require association, connectedness, and membership in a basic community to grow and achieve a sense of personal well-being. The community gives to each of its members the potential for identity, for individual power, for "response-ability" and responsibility. When various small communities are available on a large university campus, this multiplicity of reference groups can have a very positive impact on the individual. A milieu can be consciously created that uses the strong need for peer association to promote individual development and agreed upon educational goals. In many ways such creation is the essence of the student development model being proposed.

The Multi-Ethnic Program of the University of California at Davis offers an alternative environment for third-world (Asian-American, American Indian, Black, Chicano, Spanish surname, and Filipino) students who sense such a need for community. Coming from various cultural backgrounds, they are often different from the majority of university students in ways ranging from life styles and value systems to diets. For these students, the regular residence hall system has not proven successful or satisfying because they have felt forced to repress their personality characteristics and cultural values to survive in the dorms. The MEP is designed (1) to provide peer support for third-world students as they adjust to the university; (2) to generate healthy interaction between special interest groups on campus and the third-world students in residence halls; (3) to improve the multi-cultural education of all university students living on and off campus.

In March 1974, a group of Asian-American students approached the chairperson of Housing's Task Force on Residence Hall Environments and requested the formation of an all-Asian floor. With assistance from her and the assistant business manager, the proposal was broadened to include all ethnic groups. During its first year, MEP was organized and operated by students, with the help of some advisory staff and faculty members.

During the 1975–1976 school year, the Multi-Ethnic Program occupied one floor of a three-story residence hall. All but five of the students were freshmen, and all the third-world subgroups were represented, although not in proportion to their numbers in the population. Two undergraduate resident advisors lived on the floor, and a full-time professional resident director lived in the building.

The students held both formal weekly meetings and numerous informal gatherings. They also heard guest speakers, watched films, and participated in workshops and seminars on different aspects of ethnic cultures, including customs and crafts.

The program hopes to generate enough interest to keep the floor filled from year to year, produce some positive feelings toward residence hall living on the part of MEP students, and help them get over the "culture shock" of living in Davis and adjusting to university life. To measure these outcomes, the staff administers the MEP Floor Survey in January and June. The students rate the physical facilities (availability of ethnic music and literature), the group atmosphere (feeling of independence, presence of cliques, feeling of isolation from rest of campus), and the amount of social contact; they also indicate the group with which they are personally identified. A less formal evaluation tool is the staff observation at weekly meetings. The program's success is judged by the attitude changes revealed in the survey, the attendance at meetings, the number of students who sign up for the program, and the number who return for a second year.

These four programs have been presented as functional examples of how student development professionals might create milieus that require less than full campus involvement at the outset. In many cases, such activities could be initiated almost immediately because the staff, resources, and authority to begin are already available. Most institutions could implement similar pilot programs to test out their current abilities to move toward advanced-level developmental programming. Many readers will be able to identify current campus programs that reflect milieu management strategies. In all likelihood, the greater the number of such programs one can identify locally, the closer the campus is to developing a functional institutionwide program.

TECHNIQUES OF INSTITUTIONWIDE MILIEU MANAGEMENT

An ecosystem model developed by a multidisciplinary task force associated with the Western Interstate Commission for Higher Education (WICHE) is an attempt to assess (map) and construct (design) environments to produce the most compatible transactions between students and their milieu. The seven basic steps in the ecosystem design process (WICHE, 1972, p. 7) are the following: (1) designers, in conjunction with community members, select educational values; (2) values are translated into specific goals; (3) environments are planned that contain mechanisms to reach the stated goals; (4) environments are fitted to students; (5) students' perceptions of the environments are measured; (6) the behavior that results from their perceptions is monitored; (7) data on the design's success and failures, as indicated by the students' perceptions and behavior, are fed back to the designers in order that they may continue to learn about the student/environment fit and create better milieus. This model can be applied to a whole college, to specific groups on campus, and to the individual's relationship with the academic setting.

For a college community, one practical entry point is Step 5. In mapping students' perceptions of the environment, numerous assessment instruments, such as the College and University Environment Scales, the Student Reactions to College, the College Student Questionnaire, and the Institutional Goals Inventory, all published by the Educational Testing Service, are available. A fairly comprehensive assessment of all community members can provide information on matches and mismatches among the views of students, faculty members, and administrators. The next step is tying any negative perception to the policy, program, or event that is stimulating it. Then, this stimulant or referent must be redesigned to produce more favorable reactions. For those especially interested in the ecosystem model, the training manual recently published by WICHE is recommended (Aulepp and Delworth, 1976).

Developmental intervention in postsecondary educational communities has primarily taken place in residence halls, although the designs used there are useful in other settings. Four types of communities can be readily identified (Crookston, 1974). A content-centered arrangement might be a living-learning program in which students and faculty live and study specific subjects. In an environment-centered community, attempts are made to establish or

124

alter the setting to make it conducive to the expression of creative, artistic, or other particular goals. A person-centered milieu is focused on self-awareness, interpersonal relations, and life planning. And building a sense of itself is the purpose of a group-centered community. Believing that increased size and complexity tend to alienate and dehumanize students, many institutions have experimented with some form of clustering, such as gathering students in living-learning centers or small subcolleges with innovative curricula. Governance structures on campus can also contribute to milieu management. Student self-governance programs contribute to mastery and the development of autonomy and interdependence.

The following represent institutionwide programs for managed milieus.

Hood College Model. In response to the interest shown by students, as well as to their requests for help, a Three-Year Program for student development was undertaken by Hood College in Frederick, Maryland. When the model was conceived in 1973, many staff members from various student services offices (the dean of students, financial aid, counseling, health services, continuing education, student activities, career planning and placement) had a hand in its design. The plan was to move from student services to student development, from doing things for students to giving them the information and tools they need to do things themselves. The structure of the new office of student development was intended to eliminate the disadvantages of the traditional hierarchy (vertical communication, jealous guarding of tasks) but maintain the advantages of responsibility and accountability.

The model is in the form of a wheel, at whose hub is the director of student development, who serves as a clearinghouse for information and ideas, as the coordinator of activities, and as the person who maintains communication within the staff and with other college offices. The "inner ring" comprises the student development specialists, who have a wide variety of duties, and the next ring is composed of staff members who have specific responsibilities. Because the structure is somewhat ambiguous, positions and procedures are continuously redefined, and task teams form and dissolve as necessary. In the outermost circle are the students and faculty members. The faculty perspective is represented by two teachers who attend staff meetings and offer their advice. The student assistants who are employed in the office also attend these meetings to express their opinions on policies and procedures. The other means of assessing students' views is a yearly questionnaire sent to all undergraduates (residents and commuters). The results are used to measure progress and plan future directions.

A great many goals were formulated, ranging from personal objectives to broader, more group-centered aims. Among the former are: increased self-awareness, growth in independence, a better self-image, an appreciation of scholarship as a lifetime vocation, leadership development, improved communication and job finding skills, and skills for developing meaningful relations with the opposite sex. The latter include: support in defining the role of women, a dorm atmosphere that enhances academic and social learning as well as individual growth, better coordination of student organizations, family counseling, development of a grievance channel for students, employment opportunities and internships, participation in the cultural and social activities of Washington, D.C., and improved minority affairs. The goals were gathered in several categories in the three-year plan shown below.

Academic Year 1974–1975
Campus Life
Career Education and Development
Internship and Employment Opportunities
Minority Affairs
Staff Cohesiveness/Growth and Development
Support in Defining Role of Women
Academic Year 1975–1976
Closer Relationship with Students
Community Involvement
Health Management
Interaction with Area Colleges
Orientation
Practical Aspects of Living

Environmental Management

Staff Growth Conference
Academic Year 1976–1977
    Cultural, Social, Intellectual Program
    Evaluation of Dormitory Facilities
    Graduate Student Integration in Campus Life
    Off-Campus Housing

Work on these various aims continues in an unstructured way during the whole period, but the items listed under each year have priority and are being developed according to the timetable presented. The following description of the campus life programs, including comments on their status at the end of the first year, illustrates the efforts that are being made.

Campus life is a rather broad term which includes housing and its administration, nonresident students, activities, and governance. This outline expresses the objectives of the student development staff.

A. Student Resident Advisor Program
    1. Expand staff beyond original two advisors per dormitory. (One more dorm advisor and one nonresident advisor were added for second year.)
    2. Reassess and broaden job descriptions.
    3. Conduct training course for credit each year before staff is assigned. (Turned down by faculty.)
    4. Establish position of student administrative assistant to coordinate residence program under supervision of student development staff. (Still handled by a staff person.)
B. Dormitory Programming (to create an atmosphere that enhances academic, social, and personal learning—taking responsibility and initiative, making decisions, interacting with other individuals and groups)
    1. Work with house councils as instruments for implementing dorm programming. (Still at the level of getting constitutions written.)
    2. Suggest ideas to students for programs on learning, living, and recreational/entertainment.

127

C. Nonresident Student Programming (same goals as dorm programming)
   1. Expand and relocate day student facilities in Student Development Center. (Yet to be accomplished.)
   2. Offer college housing for rent to male students. (Not attained to date.)
   3. Work with officers to implement programming. (Just beginning.)
   4. Stimulate ideas for programming in areas of learning, living, and recreation/entertainment.
   5. Help students become more aware of scheduled events. (Accomplished.)
D. Governance and Activities
   1. Establish closer ties and better coordination among student organizations. (Accomplished.)
   2. Conduct team-building workshop. (Accomplished.)
   3. Offer leadership-training workshops. (Accomplished.)
   4. Present communication skills workshops.
   5. Encourage students to take over responsibility for all their publications.
   6. Publish brochure giving information on the college and describing the expectations of students. (Accomplished.)
   7. Locate student organization offices in Student Development Center. (Yet to be accomplished.)

The Hood College program represents an excellent attempt at creating an institutionwide environment conducive to the growth of all involved. It uses a vast array of campus resources and is not limited to the out-of-class life of students alone. Likewise, it seeks to respond to the developmental needs of all students, whether they be campus residents or commuters. Perhaps the most important single point to note, however, is that the program is longitudinal, with a built-in schedule. Some goals can be achieved quickly, while others take more time and some may have to be discarded—at least for the time being. Through such comprehensive, planned programming, long-range success is more likely to be achieved than it would be if the college tried to move from a traditional to a developmental approach in one fell swoop.

Environmental Management

Another technique for managing the environment falls within a competency-based model of education. Its aim is to produce a learning environment in which the desired abilities and the criteria for evaluating them are stated explicitly to all participants. Competencies are those particular verbal and nonverbal skills, actions, and attitudes that represent social, physical, emotional, and intellectual growth. Competency-based methods emphasize planning, programming, and control of the conditions in which students live and learn.

Alverno College Program. "Liberal learning in a management context" is what Alverno College in Milwaukee is attempting to achieve. Its mission is to provide learning so students can manage change successfully in their lives; become integrated, functioning humanists; acquire a transdisciplinary view of a complex and rapidly changing world; choose, plan, and design their own professional direction and career orientation; do competently what they have learned; and act as effective change agents in providing leadership in a profession, school, community, or any other type of organization that seeks to alter any of its structures.

To implement this concept, two major steps are required: first, liberal education is defined functionally as a set of student goals to be accomplished in order to graduate; and second, plans are made to achieve these goals using three strategic components—management of change, academic experience, and professional direction. The college provides careful guidance for the students in relating goals to values and career aspirations, in making maximum use of learning resources, in assessing states of development, and ultimately in earning a degree. And it promises each student that she will know what she must *do* to graduate, what available resources will give her the most help in learning how to do it, and to what extent she is, at any point, able to do it. The student can then meaningfully decide how to use her time and combine learning experiences.

Implicit in this program is a blurring of the distinction between teaching and academic advising. As one who shares the responsibility for all aspects of the student's growth, the advisor helps her develop a set of directions which can guide her present activities as well as define the future. Thus, management becomes an assumed approach to life for every student. The student inventories all the components of each objective, examines her own capacities, presents herself to the advisor for an analysis of her relevant strengths and weaknesses, designs a prescription from the alternatives available, and goes about building her skills.

At present, most of the resources available are (1) course "modules" that make explicit what kind of performance is expected for each learning experience; (2) off-campus experiential learning arrangements; or (3) individual study packets. The aim of all these resources is to integrate practice and content in a way that makes both meaningful. The criterion that faculty members apply to their instructional strategy is simple: Does it enable the student to learn? Faculty members identify at what point and by what means they can contribute most. Students may still best learn by having individual faculty members help them communicate and analyze in history or physics. Or they may fare better with faculty teams, who offer interdisciplinary approaches to such subjects as contemporary events, problem solving, social interaction, and environmental issues. Faculty members agree that each student must be able to select the mode that best suits her pace, style, and needs.

In writing, speaking, reading, listening, and social interaction labs, students can get direction and feedback. As they work on each of these skills, they discover how to make maximum use of the persons, properties, and processes that seem to be most helpful. The Media Center houses other important resources—particularly videotaping—which supplement and supplant courses so that, at a given moment, a student can find what she needs to continue developing a given competence.

As these learning activities continue to expand and become integrated, they will, by design, bridge the breaks between classes. A student in search of competence cannot wait for a given course in a given room in a given semester; she needs a variety of avenues to attain her objective, and Alverno is fast becoming the sort of environment that provides them.

The college intends that each student will develop eight kinds of competence which are essential if the woman of today is to function well both personally and professionally. These are: (1) effective communication skills; (2) strong analytical capabilities; (3) workable problem-solving skills; (4) ability to make independent judgments and decisions; (5) facility in managing healthy social interactions; (6) an understanding of the relationship between the individual and the environment; and (7) awareness and understanding of the world in which the individual lives. To achieve these aims, she needs a repertoire of ways of looking at reality, ways that go beyond the academic disciplines as we know them. By integrating academic and personal abilities within the formal curriculum, this program moves toward a more fully managed milieu.

William Rainey Harper College Program. A technique that is closely related to competency-based education and currently popular in the literature, if not in practice, is management by objectives (Odiorne, 1965). At William Rainey Harper College in Palatine, Illinois, they call it administration by objectives. According to its proponents, this approach has several benefits. First, it requires clarification of institutional goals. Since each person's objective must be related to those of the college, any school that uses the system is forced to take a new look at its basic purpose and the contributions that each person and academic unit makes to accomplishing them. An associated benefit is renewed attention to long-range planning, which otherwise tends to slip out of sight. As aims and plans are specified, it is easier to see what's important and to do away with irrelevant practices and positions. Further, communication improves, too. People understand their responsibilities more clearly, and since the emphasis is on performance and results, good work is recognized and rewarded. As a result, staff morale rises as well. And finally, the student's importance is stressed. ABO leads educators to find new ways of measuring the developmental outcomes of education and to study the impact of particular programs on students. Certainly, developing specific, measurable objectives is difficult because the "products" of education are people and evaluating their growth is a complex undertaking, but ABO at least makes a systematic effort to do so. Although primarily an administrative technique, which is dealt with in more detail in Chapter Eight, the Harper College Model has been presented here to show how MBO approaches might be used as part of a milieu management strategy.

ROLE OF THE STUDENT DEVELOPMENT EDUCATOR

To implement all these principles and techniques of environmental management, the educator must be actively involved in the whole process of education, developing productive associations with students, faculty members, administrators, and others throughout the institutional community. It is particularly important for the student affairs person to build good working relations with the faculty and to become a voting member of major governing bodies. As he or she achieves more influence on campus, the educator should be in an increasingly stronger position to bring about positive change.

This role requires several kinds of knowledge and abilities. First of all, the student affairs professional should become a competent generalist, one who has a basic understanding of the campus ecology, management theory, social systems, and the behavioral sciences. Knowledge of how the environment influences student development is extremely important because if we can anticipate how certain changes are likely to occur, we will be more able to direct them. But beyond reacting to change, the educator should understand how groups and organizations operate so that programs can be designed that act on the college as a system rather than on only one part. Some pertinent literature includes Bennis, Benne, and Chin (1969), Shein and Bennis (1965), and recent materials published by WICHE (Moore and Delworth, 1976, and Aulepp and Delworth, 1976). The educator should also be aware of other environments that students may select to complement or replace the college milieu. This knowledge can be effectively used to help them choose the setting that will be most conducive to their development at a particular time (Grant, 1972).

Despite our attempts to describe various interactions between students and their environment and to state what the educator should do about them, it is evident that we are a long way from establishing a complete theory. A great deal of research and conceptualization remains to be accomplished. None of the current theories is sufficiently comprehensive, clear, or parsimonious; nor does it include all the known findings or generate adequate guides for implementation (Walsh, 1973). The complexity of the task is challenging, for so many questions remain. For instance, how shall we determine the limits of our efforts? What is the optimum size of an organization or environment that can be managed effectively? Nevertheless, the concepts of milieu management have great potential for directing student development programming and should not be overlooked.

In what represents his last public statement to the profession, Burns Crookston (1975, p. 3) shared his view of milieu management, which seems like a fitting close for his chapter.

> *What is milieu management?* It is the systematic coordination and integration of the total campus environment—the organizations, the structures, the space, the function, the people and the relationships of each to all the others and to the whole—toward growth and development as a democratic community. In furtherance of human development theory, the relationship of the whole milieu with all its parts and vice versa must be symbiotic, or mutually enhancing or growth producing. Thus as the individual and the group contribute to the total community they give the community the capacity to create the conditions that contribute to the enhancement of the individual and the group. This symbiotic relationship of the individual to the community is the classical definition of democracy.

Chapter 7

⚔⚔⚔⚔⚔⚔⚔⚔

Evaluating Programs

Delaying evaluation until pressed for accountability by the general public, state legislatures, institutional budget administrators, or parents and students can be disastrous to any program. In fact, efforts to design programs responsive to the developmental needs of students must show that they will make a difference before new expenditures of funds can be justified. Thus, systematic evaluation is essential whether one is accountable to an external agent or not. Such evaluation calls for more than the use of rating forms to discover participants' satisfaction with a program and more than simple reports of numbers served and subjective statements about

134

staff abilities. These data alone are inadequate as bases for deciding to modify or curtail existing programs or inaugurate new ones. Evaluation must be part of program planning: it is a continuous process of delineating, obtaining, and providing information with which to judge various choices (Stufflebeam, 1971).

Often the effectiveness of a program is not examined at all, possibly because staff members have not had enough training in evaluation or because they fear that the outcomes will reflect negatively on them. Burck and Peterson (1975) have outlined four strategies that are sometimes used in the name of evaluation but that fall short of providing useful information. The "Sunshine Method" provides elaborate program advertisements with bulletin boards, colorful ads, and clever announcements while ignoring questions of quality and impact. The "Committee Method" produces a favorable attitude toward results simply because the program was a collective endeavor. Similarly, when well-intended program activities are conducted without a clear set of objectives, the evaluator uses "The Shot-in-the-Dark Method," since there are no standards for demonstrating the program's impact anyway. When the "Annointing by Authority Method" is employed, an external consultant-evaluator praises the program to the right people. Obviously, some institutions expend considerable amounts of energy on avoiding serious evaluation. This effort may perhaps be due more to a lack of staff know how than to a lack of professionalism; nevertheless, rigorous evaluation is essential to the long-term success of any program and deserves careful attention throughout.

The failure to distinguish between research and evaluation often results in the failure to collect the kinds of data needed to decide about continuing or modifying a given program. Even though they are similar in process, research and evaluation have somewhat different purposes. Research is intended to advance scientific knowledge, while evaluation is aimed at collecting information that will help immediately in making decisions (Oetting and Hawkes, 1974). In research, experiments must be planned to account for possible errors that might affect the results. Likewise, research tends to be more theory-oriented, uses more complex and exact designs, requires

135

fewer judgments by the researcher, and is more concerned with explaining and predicting phenomena. Evaluation, on the other hand, is more mission-oriented, tends to be less rigorous, and is concerned with explaining events and their relationships to established goals and objectives. In addition, since evaluation is usually accomplished on site, it cannot be as controlled as laboratory research. All in all, forcing field problems into inappropriate research molds results in frustration, which may well underlie the often obvious avoidance of evaluation (Burck and Peterson, 1975).

For student development purposes, evaluation should accomplish several goals. First, it should *test theory*. Programming should be based on student development theory that has been made concrete by assessing students' needs. The evaluative test should be a genuine effort to prove the theory wrong, for only when we attempt to prove something wrong (false) can we credibly maintain that it is right (true), since a theory can never been proven right as such. Evaluation should also *test the implementation plans*. Was the correct department, division, task team, individual, or combination assigned to produce the desired outcomes? This step tests the organizational structure as well as the collaborations which are affected within it. Likewise, was the correct student population selected, and were the strategies based on a correct interpretation of the assessment of needs? Next, the evaluator should *test the implementation tactics*. Determining whether the program's format was the best one for achieving the desired results is important, as is finding out whether appropriate publicity reached those it was intended to reach. But, more important, did the process achieve its objectives? Evaluation should *test the staff's effectiveness*. Did they have the skills necessary to accomplish the task at hand and did they effectively carry out the plans? And were the people with the best abilities chosen or were people assigned because of their positions within the organization? Finally, the evaluator should *test for goal-outcome fit*. Every evaluation should state definitely that the program's results do or do not represent achievement of the stated goal. If such a statement cannot be made, then either the evaluation procedures were inadequate or the goal was ill-defined or, perhaps, unrealistic. In either instance, the program must be judged to have been inadequately planned or implemented. This kind of evaluation is no easy task, but without its objectivity to assist us, we will never be secure in the fact that we are doing all we can to achieve our goals, nor will our institutional leaders and constituents.

In addition to the foregoing questions, four others that are closely related to student development theory should elicit important data. (1) Has the concept of continuous and cumulative growth been considered in planning the program, and how was it implemented? (2) Were developmental goals clearly stated beforehand, and were the activities directly related to these aims? (3) Was the program designed to produce the results needed and wanted by students, and what evidence indicates that these outcomes were achieved? (4) Did staff members, faculty members, and students representing different constituencies collaborate significantly in planning and implementing the program?

Still other criteria are important to consider. For instance, program goals should be consistent with institutional goals and objectives, be realizable within resource constraints, and be acceptable to the staff members who must attain them (Stimpson and Simon, 1974). Both the institution and its constituents must "own" the program if it is to succeed.

ACCOUNTABILITY

Although the kind of evaluation we've been discussing is intended to satisfy the internal requirements of a particular program—its goals and its clientele—systematic assessment procedures can also be used to respond to the demands of a larger public. An accountability system is a set of procedures that collates information about accomplishments and costs to facilitate decision making (Krumboltz, 1974). The potential advantages of such a system for student development extend beyond budgetary expediency, however. It can give student affairs professionals feedback on the results of their work, help them select strategies based at least on a demonstrated lack of failure (Popper, 1963), identify unmet developmental needs, provide evidence to support requests for additional resources, essential to attaining the goal, and supply the ammunition needed to argue for or against continuation of a particular program or approach.

The failure to create specific program goals produces vague objectives which defy evaluation. Likewise, failing to define clearly to whom we are accountable results in ambiguous program goals not clearly serving the needs of any one population. One way to overcome the first problem in developing a sound accountability system is to determine what characteristics are associated with mature development and then organize opportunities for growth. An assessment of students' needs, as mentioned earlier, gives the student development educator and program planner an excellent start. But the next step is probably more important: using the data produced by the assessment to establish realistic goals and measurable objectives. These aims should also be closely coordinated with the stated mission of the college, since applying human development theory in the postsecondary setting should definitely be part of its educational purpose.

The second problem is less easily surmounted. It requires considerable soul searching and clarification of values by all educators, for they must determine ultimate responsibility. In most instances the public, represented by the taxpayers, is identified as the entity to whom educators are to be held accountable (Bowers, 1972). Such a view subtly implies that the purpose of student development programming should be to prepare students to meet societal expectations. The National Defense Education Act, which was part of the federal government's response to the launching of the first Russian satellite, exemplifies this view. One of its purposes was to train counselors to "counsel" students into the sciences for the "public's" betterment. But the very essence of the student development approach is providing for students' needs in order to realize their full potential as persons, whether that satisfies the public or not. Can education simultaneously serve both the needs of students and the interests of society? Is manipulation of the student to conform to the expectations of others required? Can accountability be achieved by determining community consensus or by using established social or religious criteria and then making students meet them? Although the public at large, our governing bodies, and institutional leaders have important opinions that must be considered, it is the individual human beings with whom we work to whom we are ultimately answerable. To hold otherwise is to subordinate the individual to the state, an action which goes against the basic tenets on which our country was founded.

Of course, many people challenge this position, and that is as it should be. This is a philosophical issue which requires considerable dialogue and debate. But whatever stance is taken, the evaluator must settle the question of accountability, for that answer determines the evaluation criteria to be used.

Although we do not favor using a student development program to serve societal needs alone, a program evaluation should be compatible with a broader accountability system in the college. For this reason, the evaluator should talk with others about the types and forms of information they require for budgetary and other decision-making purposes. At least three kinds of accountability data could be readily developed and presented to institutional administrators: *internal data* (type and number of students participating, institutional resources used, and amount of staff time spent on a specific activity), *consumer data* (impact of program on students, faculty and staff members, and others), and *judgments* of other professionals, such as an evaluation agency or team (Trembley and Bishop, 1974). Once a decision is made about the kinds of data desired, implementing appropriate procedures for obtaining those data can be initiated.

PROCESSES AND PROCEDURES

The five steps in program development and evaluation recommended by Burck and Peterson (1975) represent a familiar cycle: assessing needs, stating goals and objectives, designing programs, revising and improving the program, and reporting program outcomes.

Assessing Needs. Several techniques can be used to analyze the needs of those expected to participate. Sometimes the program designer can simply talk to people to find out what they want to know. Usually, however, more formal procedures are desirable because of the need to conserve institutional resources and make programming as effective as possible. One method begins when the planners develop an extensive list of possible program goals and then obtain a desirability rating from a group of the proposed participants. Once these aims have been determined, another student sample completes an instrument designed to ascertain their current level of knowledge, awareness, or competence in relation to the goals. Finally, the planners select the program objectives by deciding which subjects should get the most attention and how much they can get, given the estimated resources. With this relatively simple procedure, it is possible to design a program that will actually respond to important needs, because students were involved in determining them.

Another approach is useful when a developmental task—such as becoming autonomous, improving relationships, and discovering a life purpose—has been identified but the designers do not have a clear picture of which specific needs deserve the most attention. For instance, if career development is the task, students are asked, What barriers are keeping you from making effective career-related decisions? And, What should be done to help you make those career-related decisions? Once they have answered these questions, they are split into small groups and asked to come to a consensus on each question and then to rate the importance of other groups' answers. When all groups have ranked the responses, a steering committee is appointed to sort the "barriers" and the "desires" into categories and then rewrite them into statements of needs. When this has been accomplished, each participant arranges the need statements in order of priority, and then, finally, the planners can set objectives, again adjusting them to available resources (Bank, 1974).

A number of standarized instruments can also be useful in analyzing students' needs. They include the Student Reactions to College measure (published by the Educational Testing Service), the College Student Questionnaire (Peterson, 1968), the Career Planning Program (American College Testing Program, 1976), and the Student Developmental Task Inventory (Prince, Miller and Winston, 1974). Appropriate environmental assessment instruments include the College and University Environment Scale (Pace, 1969), the Activities Index and the College Characteristics Index (Stern, 1970), and the Environmental Assessment Inventory (Conyne, 1975). Local questionnaires and other instruments can obviously be developed, too. An excellent additional source of guidance on this subject is Aulepp and Delworth (1976). The American College Testing Program also offers consultation for those interested in implementing an institutional self-study.

To base a program on untested assumptions about a given population, on the fact that another institution had success with a given program, or on an interest in experimenting with a particular developmental task is neither a good way to use resources nor good planning. Staff members must use their time and energies constructively if the students are to be truly benefited, and assessing needs as a normal part of evaluation can increase this likelihood considerably.

Stating Goals and Objectives. Statements describing specific behavioral goals are extremely desirable, but they must be reduced to measurable performance objectives. Intended outcomes determine what the program is about, where it is going, and how one knows when the objectives have been attained. Student affairs programs have been successfully using organizational objectives to guide management in recent years. For instance, the student affairs division of the University of Minnesota, Duluth, is involved in a systematic, year-long evaluation program. Both individual and staff objectives are planned and negotiated during the early summer, followed by evaluation sessions in mid-winter and again in late spring. The entire staff of a particular office, along with their university administrators, takes part in all these activities.

The purpose of this type of developmental evaluation is to help staff members improve their job performance by systematically assessing their work. Thus, *the evaluation is not an end in itself.* Such a program has a reasonable chance to succeed when the participants firmly believe that people need to know what is expected of them, that goals are more easily reached when there is a clearly de-

141

fined plan, that people are important and want to be seen as competent, that colleagues are responsible for helping each other grow as professionals, and that the task of achieving objectives is shared by staff members at all levels of the organization.

The following outcomes are expected: (1) the aims of the whole staff will be integrated with the overall mission of the university and will be understandable to students, faculty members, and administrators; (2) each staff member will accomplish the established objectives; (3) unmet objectives, and the reasons for their not being achieved, will be clearly evident to the staff; (4) intrastaff communications will be improved; (5) interdepartmental cooperation on related projects will be increased; (6) staff morale will improve; (7) individual and collective abilities will be assessed and strengthened; (8) student needs will be more effectively assessed and adequately met; and (9) the staff will achieve goals previously thought unattainable.

Initially, a series of staff workshops and intensive seminars in MBO techniques and principles were held for all student affairs staff. The group involved was not only the target of change but also the medium of change. Other advantages of the group process are the following: each individual will have the attention and recognition of peers and superiors for at least three extensive periods during the year; each member of the group experiences what it is like to be both the evaluator and the evaluatee; and the knowledge that each member of the group is responsible for his or her feelings and behavior is made evident.

The successes and failures of such a program are determined by comparing the results with the list of expected outcomes. For instance, staff morale is evaluated by such methods as having an outside person interview staff members or students. To assess the staff's competence, the perceptions of students, faculty members, and staff members are sampled, and staff accomplishments are analyzed.

Designing the Program. Activities can be based on newly created techniques derived from theory as well as on previously implemented programs with similar objectives. The preceding chapters have gone into considerable detail concerning various types of

142

designs, but the importance of outlining and carefully following procedures must be emphasized, for these are, in effect, the "lesson plans" which guide the development to be obtained. There will be nothing concrete to evaluate at the end if the plans have not been conscientiously carried out.

Improving the Program. Probably the single most important purpose of evaluation is to provide accurate information that can be used for revising the program. Both formative evaluation (Bloom, Hastings, and Madeus, 1971) and transactional evaluation (Rippy, 1973) are useful tools. Formative evaluation provides both participants and leaders with feedback information as they progress through a learning experience, while transactional evaluation assesses the adequacy of the communications among participants.

Both forms of evaluation are part of the *Colleague Evaluation Program* at El Centro College. This approach offers counselors opportunities to explore their own strengths and those of their colleagues, thus encouraging them to use their present skills more productively and to improve their abilities with the aid of the feedback they receive. This program is expected to increase communication and cooperation within the staff, encourage staff members to give more attention to setting their personal and professional goals, and increase everyone's willingness to participate in the evaluation and keep the evaluation data up to date and relevant. The program involves all counselors in an annual four-week evaluation which culminates in a half-day group discussion of the results.

A report form with no summative scale to rate counselors is used, on the premise that the most effective way to upgrade professional skills is to make suggestions for improvement rather than to use a sociometric device to compare counselors. The items evaluated include: volume of work, job knowledge and skills, personal work habits, ability to communicate understanding, team effort, professional development, and public relations abilities. Ratings are scaled from "Does not meet minimum job requirements" to "Exceeds job requirements." When a counselor calls for improvement in a colleague, written suggestions must be offered and each staff member receives a compilation of these suggestions for review before the

143

TABLE 3. Sample Accountability Report

General Goal A: Decision Making—Help Students Learn How to Make Decisions Wisely

Accomplishment			Cost		
Problem Identification	Method	Outcome	Activity	Hours	Dollars
178 seniors volunteered for vocational decision-making program; 25 were picked at random	Group counseling; vocational simulation; outside exploratory assignments	19 mastered and applied 8-step vocational decision-making process, ending with written tentative action plan; each verbalized how process could apply to new decisions; 6 verbalized process but did not apply it to own vocational decision	Questionnaire administration/analysis	4	56
			Preparation for learning activities	20	280
			Group meetings	10	140
			Job experience kits (reusable)	0	173
			Follow-up evaluation	25	350
					999

General Goal B: Raising Career Aspirations—Help Women Consider Nontraditional Alternatives

Accomplishment			Cost		
Problem Identification	Method	Outcome	Activity	Hours	Dollars
Staff meeting discussion revealed concern with limited career aspirations of women; survey showed 78% chose "housewife," "nurse," or "stewardess"	Organized 9 noon discussion groups led by career woman in community	Half of the 90 women attending 1 or more noon meetings actively explored occupational alternatives vs. 1% of nonattenders (self-selection?); attenders listed interest in 2.4 times as many occupations at end of year as at beginning, vs. 1.1 for nonattenders	Planning meetings	3	42
			Arrangements	4	56
			Discussion groups	9	126
			Evaluation	8	112
					336

NOTE: Staff limitations prevented us from reaching 153 seniors who wanted our vocational decision-making program. We can show that the program works. Let's build a case with the administration for hiring more counselors who can accomplish results for our students.
Source: Krumboltz, 1974, pp. 643–644.

group discussion session. At this meeting, the counselors talk about their personal and professional growth. Once the discussion is completed, the director may or may not be told about what happened, depending on the consensus. Through this kind of peer evaluation and feedback, both the abilities of the staff and program activities which deserve continuation or require change can be readily identified and dealt with more effectively.

Reporting the Results. At some point the evaluators must report their results to institutional leaders so that intelligent program decisions can be made in the future. Since the primary reason for collecting evaluative data is to decide how best to use institutional resources for student development, clear, nontechnical interpretations of the information are especially important. The accountability report system designed by Krumboltz (1974) is excellent (see Table 3). This report shows how the behavior of college students was modified through student development programs as well as how many students and contact hours were involved. The system associates accomplishments with costs, permitting better decisions about effective methods, staffing, student needs, and training. As Krumboltz indicates, an accountability system does not assess the value of an outcome, for it measures only its costs. The activities of the student development educator should be stated as costs, rather than as accomplishments. Time spent talking with a student, for example, is a cost; the accomplishment is what the student learns to do as a result of the program. The accountability system must be constructed to promote professional effectiveness as opposed to casting blame or punishing poor performance. The emphasis should be on diagnosis and self-improvement. In order to promote accurate evaluation, failures and unknown outcomes must be reported but never punished. In addition, the evaluation system itself must be subject to careful study and modification.

SKILLS NEEDED

A number of technical abilities are required for implementing evaluation processes (Oetting and Hawkes, 1974), although analysts do not agree on which ones the student development educator should have. A solid knowledge of research design is basic, because the best evaluation plan will often be a thorough research design. A strong background in instrument construction is desirable because a particular program will call for very specific measurements that cannot be made with existing tools. Knowing how to use unobtrusive measures and being skilled at assessing behavioral outcomes are also valuable. The evaluator especially needs the ability to obtain help from objective consultants not immediately involved with the program. An additional necessity is skill at reporting results clearly so as to communicate *what* should be done, *how* it can best be accomplished, and by *whom*. A concise booklet that outlines specific evaluative techniques has been published by the Cooperative Assessment of Experiential Learning project (Knapp and Sharon, 1975). The *Encyclopedia of Educational Evaluation* (Anderson and others, 1975) is another excellent resource, as is the previously mentioned WICHE publication by Auleppe and Delworth (1976).

Finally, it must be said that new attitudes are needed to make evaluation an integral part of student development programming. Administrators and staff members must overcome their defensiveness and focus on developing ways to compensate for flaws in current procedures. They should also give some attention to ethical issues, such as denying service to control groups and applying pressure to participate in evaluation processes. A serious professional problem results from ignoring many programs in which things are done to or for people who have little knowledge of what effects the treatment will have (Oetting and Hawkes, 1974). Student affairs workers must guarantee, to the best of their ability, that the programs offered are appropriate to the needs of those who participate. Evaluation is essential if individual staff members and teachers are to successfully perform at higher levels of competence in their developmental work with college students.

For too long student affairs workers and others within the academic community have relied on subjective judgments about what kinds of developmental programming students need and about whether or not those needs have been adequately met by the available opportunities. Although a refined sensitivity to the needs and expectations of students, along with the ability to respond effectively, is an extremely desirable attribute for anyone wishing to help others grow, this is not enough to produce a successful student development program. No matter how long one has been working with students, there is much to be gained from including a reasonable number of "hard-nosed," objective evaluation procedures within all programs efforts, whether they be small, individualized activities or multi-faceted campuswide projects. The all too familiar "lip service approach" to evaluation reveals a significant shortcoming that does little to enhance confidence in the student affairs staff and its programs. Including carefully planned and executed evaluation procedures as a normal part of a student development program may not guarantee success, but it will almost surely result in the establishment of significantly more effective methods for identifying and meeting students' needs. And that is what student development programming is really all about.

Chapter 8

☙☙☙☙☙☙☙

Organizational Context

A student development program or activity can be initiated in just about any setting if an energetic person has the essential knowledge and abilities and the freedom to maneuver within the system. But such a program may easily come and go without causing much of a ripple, much less making waves, in the college or even in its own unit. To prevent this occurrence, the whole institution must be committed to the goal of student development. For without the interest and backing of most members of the academic community, there can be little hope of achieving any large success.

Hurst and others (1973) illustrate this point in their description of the creation of an office of student development which was later disbanded. Although management shortcomings contributed greatly to its demise, the absence of supporting attitudes and activities certainly hindered the growth of the student development philosophy on that particular campus. It's clear that although increasing numbers of institutions have launched isolated programs within this model, very few have attempted a major reorganization to implement it on a comprehensive scale.

Before we can bring about the necessary changes—in both the student affairs organization and the institution as a whole—a careful look must be taken at the existing structures and processes to chart the future that we would like to see. To this end, the burgeoning literature on organizational development must be considered.

The concept of organizational development is no less complex than that of its human development counterpart; in fact, human groups are often likened to individual beings. For instance, Lippitt and Schmidt (1967) have outlined three developmental stages of organizations (see Table 4). In this context, most student affairs operations would seem to be moving through the second phase of youth and into the early phase of maturity. Although people in this field are still seeking to gain a good reputation and develop pride, they are also beginning to achieve uniqueness and adaptability. The proposals in this book, for example, are related to key issue number five, "whether and how to change."

Both humans and their organizations are dynamic bodies that constantly grow and adapt. Gardner (1965) suggests that perhaps what every organization really needs is a department of self-renewal which would view the whole as a system in need of continuing innovation. From this standpoint, the purpose of organizational development is to find the best ways of using human and material resources to solve institutional problems and strengthen operations. As Golembiewski (1972) points out, OD programs have several distinguishing features. They involve some meaningful system of work and they are planned and managed by the top responsible officials, who are committed to them as long-term efforts. Their aim is to improve the effectiveness of the organization by focusing on interpersonal and group processes and by giving its members opportunities to learn through direct action and experience.

149

TABLE 4. Stages of Organizational Development

Developmental Stage	Critical Concern	Key Issues	Consequences If Concern Is Not Met
BIRTH	1. To create a new organization	What to risk	Frustration and inaction
	2. To survive as a viable system	What to sacrifice	Death of organization Further subsidy by "faith" capital
YOUTH	3. To gain stability	How to organize	Reactive, crisis-dominated organization Opportunistic, rather than self-directing, attitudes and policies
	4. To gain reputation and develop pride	How to review and evaluate	Difficulty in attracting good personnel and clients. Inappropriate, overly aggressive, and distorted image building
MATURITY	5. To achieve uniqueness and adaptability	Whether and how to change	Unnecessarily defensive or competitive attitudes, diffusion of energy Loss of most creative personnel
	6. To contribute to society	Whether and how to share	Possible lack of pupil respect and appreciation Bankruptcy or profit loss

Adapted from: Lippitt and Schmidt, 1967, p. 109.

Organizational Context

The system concept is central. When the organization is seen as a living whole whose parts are interlocked in complex patterns, then it can no longer be only a group of functions or a hierarchy of people in boxes. If we want to alter or develop a particular unit, all its actual and possible ties to the other parts have to be considered—certainly not an easy task. The field of systems analysis has grown in response to this need. To move the organization in the desired direction, the analyst first must define the parts, understand their interactions, and explain the processes through which they are integrated (Hoberstroh, 1965). The basic units—including individuals, formal and informal relations, managerial styles, and the physical setting—are integrated by means of communications, decision-making procedures, and the tendency of a system to maintain a steady state or balance. Because all the parts interact with other subsystems both in and outside the organization's boundaries, planning should not be undertaken only by presidents and deans but by all the affected members in collaboration.

This systematic way of looking at complex problems has been influential in the development of another planning strategy, management by objectives, which was briefly outlined earlier. Its application in five colleges and universities is described in a book by the National Laboratory for Higher Education (Heaton, 1975), which is acting as a clearinghouse for sharing MBO activities within the higher education community. Another recent publication, *MBO Goes to College* (Deegan and Fritz, 1975), is based on the contention that "higher education needs management even more than money" (p. 5).

In capsule form, to manage by objectives means using a developmental contract to which each member of the system, including the principal officer, is a party. The setting of organizational goals and priorities usually occurs annually. Each individual and subgroup evaluates what has previously been accomplished and sets objectives for the year ahead. Then these objectives are collected by a "goals and priorities" team which determines the overall aims. A written objectives "contract" can then be articulated between each staff member and the unit head. By using these established priorities

151

to place people and material within the system, the managers can allocate resources more appropriately than can their counterparts in more traditional systems. Thus, MBO is supposed to be more productive than a system which attempts to force goals to fit an existing structure. Individual staff members should begin to function more effectively because they are carrying out responsibilities of their choice rather than arbitrary work assignments. Broad ownership of the goals is the key: the more individual members have a voice in the decisions made, the more likely they are to commit themselves to achieving the organization's objectives.

As its name implies, management by objectives is suitable for any organization, with or without student development purposes. Although subunits can use this technique, it is more effective when the total institution accepts the concept. Several caveats are in order, however. The process looks simple on paper but usually takes longer to implement than the planners anticipated, often several years. And if the staff members do not have the necessary expertise, they should definitely get help from a consultant. Even with the best intentions, there may well be some hurt feelings along the way, because MBO calls for new behavior and explicit assessment of performance by all concerned. Nonetheless, MBO does have the potential to make a student development approach more effective. At the very least it builds solid communications among the participants.

It is quite apparent that well-managed, dynamic organizations that are satisfying their clients and providing a sense of achievement for those rendering the service tend to elicit more trust among coworkers as well as more open and honest communication. When these factors are present, staff members are likely to operate more consistently within the achieved power of the organization, exhibit less dependence on the formal organizational power, and generally become more aware of both the internal and external developments that affect the group as a whole. In addition, staff members more often listen to all their colleagues within the organization, develop an influence system, and require the leader to understand that he or she cannot avoid ultimate responsibility for the functioning of the entire unit (Hill, 1974).

Organizational Context

The main reason for expending time, energy, and money on organizational development is to create and maintain a healthy organization. What does such a creature look like? One portrait is presented by Fordyce and Weil (1971, pp. 11–13), who describe seven important characteristics:

(1) Objectives are widely shared by the members and there is a strong and consistent flow of energy toward those objectives.

(2) People feel free to signal their awareness of difficulties because they expect the problems to be dealt with and they are optimistic that they can be solved.

(3) Problem solving is highly pragmatic. In attacking problems, people work informally and are not preoccupied with status, territory, or second-guessing "what higher management will think." The boss is frequently challenged. A great deal of noncomforming behavior is tolerated.

(4) Who makes the decisions, and when, is determined by such factors as the members' abilities, sense of responsibility, and work load; the availability of information; the need to decide at a particular time; and the requirements of professional and management development. The organizational level of the participants is not a factor.

(5) When there is a crisis, the people quickly band together in work until the crisis departs.

(6) Conflicts are considered important parts of decision making and personal growth. They are dealt with effectively, in the open. People say what they want and expect others to do the same.

(7) Risk is accepted as a condition of growth and change.

Using indicators such as these, the evaluator should not have much difficulty determining whether an organization is in good health, and most organizations would benefit from such an assessment activity.

PRINCIPLES OF A STUDENT DEVELOPMENT ORGANIZATION

These theories and practices, which are generally applicable to many types of groups, can be incorporated in building the foundation of an ideal student development organization. One useful set of principles has been formulated by the ACPA Conference on Organizing for Student Development, which was held in Overland Park, Kansas, in February 1976. Although many of these statements recapitulate concepts found throughout this book, they bear repeating in this context. The conference participants concluded, first, that the self-renewing organization should set goals and make decisions that are congruent with the mission of the college. Second, since all the components of the system are connected and interdependent, any planned change will touch everyone in some way. Therefore, the planners must make sure that all the members understand what the proposed change is supposed to accomplish and that they share a commitment to it. Third, all available resources— physical, financial and human—should be integrated so that the organization can respond effectively to current needs as well as plan for the future. Fourth, the decision makers must establish an open communication system in which every participant gives and receives timely and accurate information. Fifth, the organization should have regular evaluation procedures to assess both its means and its ends. And finally, this healthy organization should have a climate that stimulates and supports personal and professional development by all its members.

Crookston (1972b) makes some related recommendations. In addition to advocating a free flow of data, which leads to realistic goals and sound decisions, he believes that power should be distributed among the members of the developmental organization. And thus the authority to make most of those decisions should be given to those who are closest to the sources of information. When each member shares in the development and rewards of the operation, the best talents and energies of all can be devoted to achieving the goals of the group. The organization must also be flexible and able to adjust quickly to meet changing situational demands. He further suggests that the leaders be trained by specialists and have set terms of office so that they will be less likely to increase their power bases or cling to the status quo.

Many of these principles and recommendations may seem

impossible, yet such ideals have a rightful place in our vision. We need to know where we are trying to go even while we recognize the perils of the journey. Consideration of the following propositions should make the going seem a little more realistic.

Collaboration among student affairs staff members, faculty members, and students is essential to the success of the student development program. The cooperative relationships may be quite simple and informal: a staff person assists teachers as a resource for academic courses or helps student groups organize community projects. Or the collaboration may be quite complex and formal: representatives of the three groups establish an academic department to offer personal development courses or create a center for student development or institutional assessment and self-renewal. Faculty members may take part in residence hall and orientation programs, and student affairs workers may become regular instructors or members of teaching teams. Many members of the educational community may act as consultants for a variety of programs. Students may well serve on task teams with members of the faculty and staff to seek alternative avenues for achieving the institutional mission. In effect, by modeling interdependent and goal-directed behavior, every collaboration furthers the goal of student development.

The institution's commitment to student development is directly proportional to the number of these collaborative links between the student affairs staff and the faculty. Although these two groups have cooperated on some programs on most campuses, full collaboration is generally the exception rather than the rule. To some extent, institutional programs have been dividing the student into parts and competing for control. This separation and competition must be rejected by any college that truly wishes to serve the whole student.

The flexibility and efficiency of the student affairs staff is increased when every member can handle the basic procedures for helping students to develop and each is excellent in at least one area. Obviously, as their abilities increase, so does the success of their programs and their personal satisfaction. Staff development programs to provide and improve needed skills are necessary, especially because

155

preservice training courses too seldom help the prospective professional become competent in more than a few areas. And once the student affairs staff members become equipped to direct all the tasks of student development, they should play a significant role in promoting the staff development of all the college's employees (Creamer, 1975).

The success of a student developmental program is not totally dependent on the institution's formal organizational structures; in fact, informal arrangements that cross departmental lines are frequently more productive. Often the participants assume that a successful program must have formal support, but rigid adherence to the established structure is usually limiting. Creative and flexible programs grow best from the fertile minds of individuals unencumbered by strictly enforced hierarchies. If a new approach fails to help students meet their developmental needs, it can be easily discarded and replaced if it is not too firmly entrenched. If the experiment stands the test of time, it may then be appropriately institutionalized. Good management is essential, for only when the risks are lowered and innovative staff members are rewarded can genuine creativity be exhibited. Fostering informal collaborative endeavors which may blossom into comprehensive programs, or be withdrawn as necessary, is a most effective way to use human resources, and good managers know this. Thus, although the support from the upper administrative levels is still extremely important, much of value can result from encouraging informal interactions within the institution.

STRUCTURES PRESENT AND FUTURE

As these four propositions imply, the key to a successful student development program is the imaginative and efficient use of available resources, not the organizational structure within which it operates. Nevertheless, the structure does influence programming, and converting from a traditional student affairs format to the proposed student development approach will very likely require some alterations in the existing organization. According to a survey made by Crookston and Atkyns (1974), student affairs divisions around the country are arranged in three ways. By far the most common is the centralized line-staff structure, found in approximately 80 percent of the institutions (see Figure 2). In this situation, staff mem-

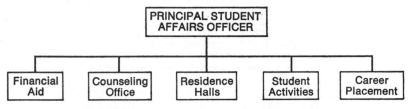

FIGURE 2. Line-Staff Structure of Student Affairs

bers use a narrow range of skills to perform a single function, and they often have few formal relations with each other, not to mention individuals and programs outside the student affairs division. Of course, both informal and formal collaborations are possible, but the focus on specialization tends to discourage them.

As more student affairs workers become adept at goal setting, assessment, and other skills required for student development, the internal organization tends to move toward what Crookston and Atkyns found to be the second most prevalent structure (11 percent of the institutions surveyed), the decentralized, multiple-program arrangement (see Figure 3). A still simpler, two-part version (1.3

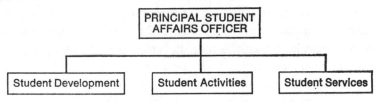

FIGURE 3. Line-Staff Structure with Three Subdivisions

percent of the institutions surveyed) has recently appeared and may well grow in popularity (see Figure 4). Both these decentralized structures tend to have "second echelon" leaders who supervise

157

their units while the principal officer concentrates on planning and coordinating the overall operation. Both give particular and formal attention to student development programming. Since cooperation and collaboration are intentional parts of the system, rather than the result of haphazard associations, teamwork is likely to replace competition or isolated functioning.

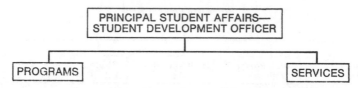

FIGURE 4. Line-Staff Structure with Two Subdivisions

The present structure of student services has been analyzed in several other ways, too. For instance, Hershenson (1970) describes four groups of functions. The *internal coordinating functions* are performed by such persons as the principal student affairs officer and the director of student records, who integrate and service the other three groups. The *orienting functions,* including recruiting, admissions, and orientation and testing programs, are concerned with clarifying and encouraging relationships among students, other inhabitants of the academic environment, and people in the community at large. The *supportive functions* are undertaken in such places as health services centers, student activities facilities, and campus residence halls; their purpose is to meet the physical and emotional needs of students so that they can get the most from the intellectual experience of college. And the *educative functions* are those co-curricular activities—remedial education, tutorial programs, student judiciary programs, student government and student volunteer services programs, for example—which aim to produce learning directly or to assist formal instruction. It's clear that such a comprehensive structure requires staff members with many abilities, and continuing training programs should be available to assist them.

Chandler (1973) proposes a tripartite arrangement, which includes a managerial-service section to handle admissions, financial aid, housing, and placement; a student development section, which takes care of counseling, student activities, advising of foreign students, community service, volunteer programs, and other student development efforts; and a judicial-control section for matters related to student conduct, discipline, and control. Chandler believes such a structure is necessary during the transition stage before the student development model can be implemented throughout the institution. This approach might well fit easily into the organizational structure represented in Figure 4.

The structure suggested by Prior (1973), who advocates two subdivisions, is also similar to the third type identified by Crookston and Atkyns. The first, the Department of Student Development, would assume the clearly educative responsibilities, such as counseling, psychological, and health services; advising of international students; academic advisement and tutorial programs; testing, measurement, and research; freshmen orientation; student activities programs; and special programs and projects (for example, peer counseling, leadership training, sensitivity training, and personal development courses). The second, the Office of Student Management, would handle such administrative matters as student rights, responsibilities, and discipline; communication between students and the administration; campus security and safety; and maintenance and security activities associated with student events and the facilities used for them. The primary purpose of such a reorganization would be to erase misperceptions of the role of student development educators and thereby prevent false expectations about what they can and should do. Under such a structure the only person on the campus *responsible* and *accountable* for a student's behavior is the student, not the student affairs workers. And thus the educative aspects of student development work are no longer directly linked to or identified with handling campus crises and problems. This clarification of roles would certainly be a move in the right direction, for student affairs administrators must become educators and begin to see themselves as having less responsibility for controlling students and more for aiding students' development.

Harvey (1974) predicts that over the next twenty years the

159

distinction between educational administration and student affairs administration will blur as higher education becomes recommitted to developing the whole student and as faculty members reassume certain functions which have been delegated to student personnel workers. Even now, student services are being defined less by office and more by function.

A creative approach to organizing for student development is the SASCH program at Trenton State College. SASCH is an acronym for Student Activities, Student Center, and Housing, working in collaboration to achieve common aims. The three overall goals of SASCH are (1) to develop community identity among all the components of SASCH by offering small group programs with a community emphasis; (2) to develop governance and policy formation (decision making) techniques that guarantee the participation of all members, moving from staff decisions to student decisions or shared decisions; (3) to develop an outreach program that involves as many students as possible. The key to this program is breaking away from the traditional formal structure and providing formal links with those student development programs which deal with students in groups. The SASCH departments have been pulled together more closely under the Group Student Development Philosophy, which is based on the belief that students naturally form into primary groups that fulfill their basic needs for security, belonging, acceptance, affection, and adequacy. Programs of SASCH departments focus on work with student groups, therefore, and on accomplishing the three goals.

A model that has great potential as a guide to implementing the student development approach throughout the college is depicted in Figure 5. Although programs are coordinated by a central office, interactions among staff members and programs are both possible and desirable (as is signified by the arrows and broken lines). In each of the four developmental areas, all appropriate strategies are used to achieve their specific goals. Such a structure would bring about an interdependent and collaborative educational community in which the growth of the whole person is intentionally pursued by all its members.

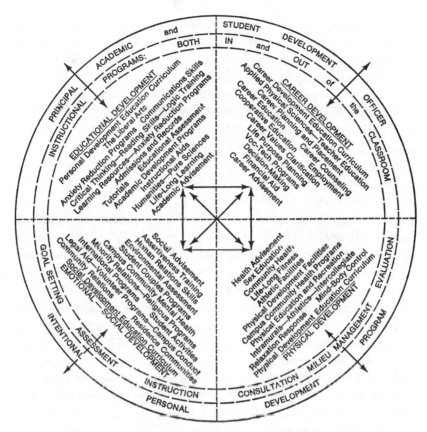

FIGURE 5. Integrated Student Development Organization

Source: Based upon an organizational structure created during the ACPA Organizing for Student Development Conference in February 1976.

PLANNED ORGANIZATIONAL DEVELOPMENT

Even the most thoughtful, systematic, and well-tested developmental plans may fail because they have so many variables. As McDaniel noted (1975, p. 8), "even when people want it very badly, [change] often gets ground up in the system" and things end up the same as they always were. One of the many factors that dis-

161

courage attempts to introduce new ideas is the unpredictable nature of interactions between persons and their environment. Another is the inexact character of communication among separate beings who have unique perceptions and feelings. Lippitt (1973, p. 3) illustrated these points when he wrote: "People within the same group or organization may not be aware of the supposedly shared goals of change. Change goals may differ in clarity, degree of acceptance, attainability, duration, and relationship with other aspects of society. The motivations of the participants in planned change may differ drastically." A further impediment, in the case of academic institutions, is their built-in resistance to change and their incoherence: "the American college or university is a prototypic organized anarchy. It does not know what it's doing. Its goals are either vague or in dispute. Its technology is familiar but not understood. Its major participants wander in and out of the organization. These factors do not make a university a bad organization or a disorganized one; but they do make it a problem to describe, understand, or lead" (Cohen and March, 1974, p. 3). Anyone who wishes to initiate planned development within such a setting must be aware of its idiosyncrasies.

Perhaps an example of an aborted reorganization effort would be helpful at this point. As mentioned briefly at the beginning of this chapter, Hurst and others (1973) describe both the process and the outcome of one institution's attempt to restructure its operation by creating an office of student development. This office was supposed to combine residence education and housing, the student center, the student services office, and the counseling center, all of which had been independent units reporting directly to the dean of students. Now they were to report to the director of the new comprehensive office, who would in turn report to the dean of students. During planning, there was a great deal of talk and little action, even resistance when structural alterations seemed imminent. The threat appeared greatest for those whose jobs were closely tied to the philosophy of *in loco parentis* and those who feared being engulfed by the counseling center, which was the source of the reorganization plan. During transition and implementation, a good deal of ambiguity arose both from sharing responsibilities for programs and from cutting across traditional departmental lines. Some were uncertain about the channels of communication and others were fearful about whether the skills they had acquired over the years would continue to be appropriate and whether the personal authority they had achieved would be lost. Lower echelon staff, such as residence hall personnel, felt that those who had concocted the student development idea were living in an ivory tower and were not aware of the many difficulties faced by those attempting to implement the program with students. Problems also arose from the interplay among the variables of organizational structure, individual personalities, past expectations, and resistance to change. During the summer following the reorganization, the dean who had provided the impetus for the restructuring retired, and the new leadership reestablished the former departmental structure.

Obviously, organizational development is neither simple nor easy. Yet unless colleges and universities keep trying, they will be unable to meet ever-changing demands and their continuing prosperity will be in doubt. What can be done to overcome the barriers to successful change? After assessing the failure of their venture, Hurst and his colleagues determined that the restructuring could have been achieved with less anxiety and stress and more internal and external support if nine basic actions had been taken: (1) Involve all staff members who are affected by the organization, especially those who must implement it. (2) Assure the participants that present programs and personal skills are valued and that any modifications will be based on careful evaluation and phased in slowly. (3) Design a gradual shift to new authority patterns, and outline long-term transition plans for all to understand. (4) Make sure that communication channels are open in all directions; feedback "up the system" should be planned and not left to chance. (5) Initiate intense programs of public relations throughout the institution to facilitate understanding of the alterations being implemented. (6) Make sure that new tasks and responsibilities associated with the planned change are not perceived as extra work. (7) Reassure all members of the organization that their voices will be heard. (8) Pay close attention to the personal needs of those involved. (9) Allow sufficient time for working through problems so that the new organization will survive and prosper.

An essential first step in organizational development is to try to analyze the problem clearly. As the foregoing story shows, all the possible difficulties cannot be known at the beginning; nevertheless, an assessment should be made. Lewin's concept of the force-field analysis (1936) can be useful for this purpose. He postulated that change takes place when the driving forces and the restraining forces in any situation are no longer in balance. So, in planning, the idea is to identify all the relevant forces and then increase the drivers, decrease the restrainers, or combine the two. Crookston and Blaesser (1962) applied these theories in designing an approach to change in a college. They believed that the use of planning strategies can offset the ways change has typically occurred in college student personnel programs, such as by administrative fiat, staff turnover, financial alterations, recommendations from others, or pressure-group demands.

Seven general strategies for mobilizing the student affairs subsystem for change and renewal have been suggested by Shaffer (1973), strategies which might be used to increase the driving forces or decrease the restraining forces. First, improve staff meetings by limiting the "administrivia" and holding substantive discussions on the relationship between theory and practice, and involve the staff in policy formulation and decision making. Second, make memorandums, position papers, and research reports that define impending issues a normal part of the operation to head off emotionally motivated, expedient actions and decisions. Third, initiate self-studies and problem-solving conferences concerning student development issues on campus. Fourth, use off-campus consultants effectively to help promote objectivity in staff deliberations. Fifth, encourage greater institutional response to and involvement in off-campus community activities. Sixth, educate and sensitize the student affairs staff to both the formal and informal governance structures and seek ways to have an influence at all levels. Finally, build a realistic power base, using knowledge of the political subsystems to guide institutional behavior in significant ways.

Organizational Context

A more comprehensive model is proposed by Blocher (1975), who combines systems theory and "change agent" concepts, both of which are well suited to higher education (see Figure 6). Blocher stresses that before developmental agents take any action, they should clearly understand their own drives, needs, values, and purposes, as well as those of the system. For they are, after all, part of

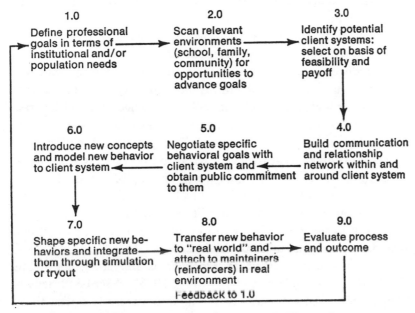

1.0
Define professional goals in terms of institutional and/or population needs

2.0
Scan relevant environments (school, family, community) for opportunities to advance goals

3.0
Identify potential client systems: select on basis of feasibility and payoff

6.0
Introduce new concepts and model new behavior to client system

5.0
Negotiate specific behavioral goals with client system and obtain public commitment to them

4.0
Build communication and relationship network within and around client system

7.0
Shape specific new behaviors and integrate them through simulation or tryout

8.0
Transfer new behavior to "real world" and attach to maintainers (reinforcers) in real environment

9.0
Evaluate process and outcome

Feedback to 1.0

FIGURE 6. Blocher's Model for Facilitating in Human Systems

Source: Blocher, 1975, p. 163.

that network, and their transactions within it affect the balance of the structure just as much as anyone else's.

Once the overall goals are defined and comprehended, the agents search for potential situations and persons with which to work to achieve the desired ends. As they look for a way to be useful, they might well consider Blocher's advice: "the way to begin to help any human system is to listen to it and help it listen to itself" (p. 165). To achieve this, they need to build communication and relationship networks within the system. Then they can begin negotiations over specific behavioral objectives with the various participants. Since development is much more likely to occur when all the members understand and agree on their purposes and the means to reach them, and when they commit themselves publicly to these aims, it behooves the agent to spend ample time in working through the expectations and contingencies with all concerned. Lack of a clear and accepted agreement is invariably a harbinger of some degree of failure.

After negotiations are completed, the selected developmental plans and strategies are implemented. As new concepts and models are introduced into the system, the agent should keep in mind that all persons have a limited tolerance for ambiguity and need time to assimilate new ideas and behaviors. They also need supervised practice with their newly acquired attitudes and skills in a secure and nonthreatening setting, as well as appropriate rewards and reinforcers to help them transfer what they've learned to the everyday work world (Miller, 1974). Nearly any goal worth accomplishing requires considerable effort on the part of those involved and the failure of agents for development to systematically "touch all the bases" will probably result in the game's being lost or, at the very least, carried into extended and expensive "extra innings."

A construct related to Blocher's is the ecosystem model (WICHE, 1972; Aulepp and Delworth, 1976), described briefly in Chapter Six. "An ecosystem is one in which there is a true transaction between mutually dependent partners, with the assumption that either may change so that mutual benefit may result" (Banning and Kaiser, 1974, p. 370). A telling argument for a shift to this approach is that the focus of much student personnel activity over the years has been on helping people adjust to the present structure, rather than on analyzing the nature of that environment. As a result, student personnel workers may well have been accommodating a noneducational environment as willing, though perhaps naive, participants. Thus, today's development planner must not accept the system at face value but seek to design milieus which will foster educational growth and development in those who inhabit them.

Although both the systems models presented above have

grown out of the "helping professions," there is no reason that they should not be used by higher education administrators concerned with institutional development and renewal. However, they do call for systematic change, and change of any kind is seldom a pleasing prospect to anyone. The establishment of a development-engendering organization, then, even though its constituents generally agree that it is important and desirable, is no easy task. Even so, higher education must move in this direction, because a healthy organization promotes healthy growth in its members. When institutional goals, functions, and resources are committed to the development of the whole person, the results will benefit all people.

Those who have helped create the model outlined in this book firmly believe that the student affairs profession can and must have a significant part in this educational enterprise, along with faculty members, administrators, and students. Only through collaborative efforts among all subunits within the community may we hope to achieve this "not-so-impossible dream." Higher education leaders and subordinates alike have the potential to make intentional human development a reality. And developing organizations designed to achieve that outcome is an excellent way to begin.

Chapter 9

❧❧❧❧❧❧❧❧

Integrating Programs

Going to college still offers unique opportunities to those who want to further their development in the adult years. Nearly half the young people in our society decide to continue their education at some kind of postsecondary institution, and many older adults are returning or starting college for the first time. Why are they seeking higher education? Many have clear life goals or specific, short-term career objectives to which college is the appropriate avenue. Others go because they have no other concrete plans or responsibilities after secondary school, because they have heard that a higher education is important to succeed in life, because parents and others expect them to, because they are trying to find themselves as

168

adult human beings, or because . . . Although their reasons can be categorized, it's also fair to say that each student brings a unique set of characteristics and purposes which influence his or her interactions with the institutional environment. And, as stated before, those interactions are what produce the educational outcomes, the growth that everyone desires and to which they are entitled. Since the resources available in the environment similarly influence what students can do, they are handicapped if a broad range of stimulating programs and opportunities is not provided. Thus, only by systematically organizing the academic milieu can their development be guided adequately.

The integrated philosophy and processes advocated throughout this book are designed to create that developmental environment and provide those opportunities. The cement that holds it all together is one shared belief: the mission of the college is to educate the whole student and not only his or her intellect. Agreement on this principle is manifested in the way personal development goals are woven into the formal academic fabric of the institution and the way all the educators and staff members collaborate to encourage students' growth. Programs are usually built to meet basic human needs, as well as the special needs of the diverse student groups on a particular campus. Sometimes physical, social, and emotional learning can be gained through regular instruction and receive academic credit. Other opportunities for personal development which do not lend themselves as well to formal teaching are offered without formal academic credit, but are just as important. To record the benefits of these "nonintellectual" experiences, a developmental transcript is a valuable complement to an academic transcript. It indicates both the kinds of experiences students have had and the developmental skills and abilities they have acquired. Only when institutions assess and recognize the essential personal learning that results from college will they truly be able to determine whether or not they are meeting the criteria for educating the whole person.

The type of institution in which an intentional student development program is implemented may be less important to its success or failure than the attitudes of the participants and the communication flow they have established. A small two-year college may have an advantage over a large university in maintaining that flow, but size alone is not the telling point. What is significant is the level of agreement on the educational mission and the means to implement it. If there is little consensus, a comprehensive program of student development, or any other program for that matter, is unlikely to become an integral part of the institution. Of course, agreement alone will not guarantee successful integration either, but lack of such consensus may well promote failure.

The impetus for establishing an intentional program for the development of students may come from a number of sources within the academic community. Quite logically, staff members of centers for counseling and campus mental health often take the initiative, and thus many of our examples have been derived from their efforts. But the spark could come just as well from the faculty or any other community members. In fact, the latter would be a welcome sign that the student development philosophy was spreading.

Since the examples offered so far were designed to illustrate particular aspects of the proposed student development model, they may have seemed like bits and pieces. This chapter seeks to eliminate any impression of fragmentation by presenting wholes— three comprehensive programs that represent systematic attempts to implement the student development approach on a large scale.

PROGRAM ONE

The University Counseling Center at Colorado State University, Fort Collins, has developed an "Approach to Services and Programs Founded on a Systematic Developmental Model." Its targets are individual students, faculty, and staff members, primary groups, campus organizations, the institution, and the larger community.

Rationale. The human characteristics that students bring to the university environment and the interaction between the two influence and produce the results of higher education and represent the basic variables involved in the postsecondary experience. It is

170

the institution's responsibility to establish programs which stress self-development. Preventive and developmental programs as well as traditional remedial efforts should help students achieve their personal and academic potential through direct services to individuals and groups or through consultation and outreach to the university as an institution.

Goals. (1) To provide students with those skills, attitudes, and resources required for maximum utilization of and success in the learning environment. (2) To enhance, modify, and contribute to the university environment according to established principles of learning and human development. (3) To continually evaluate the effectiveness of programs offered and to conduct research regarding the needs of students as they interact with the university environment.

Specific Programs and Objectives. Using a three-dimensional model of counselor functioning (Morrill, Oetting, and Hurst, 1974), five major components have been established: personal development, staff development, testing services, consultation and training, and research and evaluation. Under these headings are offered: (1) individual counseling, group counseling, behavior therapy services, and developmental programs; (2) inservice training and internship programs; (3) UCC client testing, national testing, and university testing; (4) campus consultation services, volunteer training programs, and a crisis center; and (5) environmental assessment and program evaluation.

(1) The personal-social counseling deals with such matters as loneliness, anxiety, conflicts in relationships, sexual concerns, marital problems, role conflicts, and family stress. The vocational-educational counseling is available to help students choose an academic major, select a career, and discuss related issues. Group programs ranging from problem-oriented therapy groups to developmentally oriented growth experiences provide opportunities for self-exploration and directed action within a group setting. Women's groups help their members deal with conflicts or questions about their self-concept and sex-role identity. In the men's groups, males explore their emotions and relationships with women. And general growth groups help individuals learn to acknowledge and express

171

their emotions in positive ways. Students who are anxious about taking tests, public speaking, or studying mathematics may obtain anxiety-reduction treatment to feel more relaxed and thereby improve their performance in these problem situations. Another offering is the Social Interaction Training Workshop designed to teach social skills to students having difficulty in establishing heterosexual relationships. Training groups are also available to help students become more assertive. Among the developmental programs are career development modules that give students a chance to explore various educational plans and establish realistic goals. In the life planning workshops, students try to establish meaningful personal and career goals by becoming more aware of themselves, their interests, and their personal objectives. A people-to-people program is available to help individuals learn to meet people, make friends, get closer to others, and deal with their sexuality. And through the student-couples seminar program, student pairs are given opportunities to learn to function effectively together as partners.

(2) Inservice programs for the counseling center staff are concerned with new therapeutic techniques and psychological theories that might be appropriate for working with students. Regularly scheduled staff conferences on a variety of topics related to counseling concepts and interventions also provide inservice training. An internship program gives predoctoral interns a year's professional work at the Center. Qualified counselors in training may also get practical experience in programs offered by the Center.

(3) The following testing services are available: administration and processing of all psychological tests for UCC clients; coordination of all national testing programs; administration of high school equivalancy General Educational Development Tests; academic services for the faculty, including scoring of classroom tests; administration of challenge examinations for credit for selected university courses.

(4) Consultation teams of different sizes, composed primarily of UCC staff members who have the abilities to handle a particular task, carry out a variety of responsibilities. They respond to requests from the faculty and staff for help with assessment, organizational

development, outreach programming, or other mental health efforts. They publicize relevant survey information regarding student and environmental characteristics which has been collected and analyzed. And they train student affairs workers in consultation skills. In addition, the teams work with students living in residence halls and their advisors. They offer preventive and developmental programs for students; give inservice programs for staff members on such topics as depression, referral procedures, anxiety, academic difficulties, and social inhibition; and, when necessary, help the staff handle crises. In the academic domain, the teams assist faculty members by training students to use small group discussions as an effective supplement to the lecture technique. Through group participation, students learn to accept more responsibility for their own learning.

Other consultation efforts involve the RoadHouse Crisis/Information-Calling Center, the Office of Women's Programming, and minority relations work. A person who is experiencing a crisis may receive emergency aid in the form of a sympathetic ear, problem-solving help, and referrals from volunteers trained and supervised by the UCC staff. Consultants also share information and resources on women's issues and are available as joint sponsors of specific programs concerning women's needs. Consultation teams serve minority students through special outreach programs designed to develop their potential. And team members establish programs to foster awareness in the community of minority group contributions, feelings, and needs. They also help to create a university and community environment in which minority students can live and study comfortably.

The Counseling Center increases its services to students by teaching student volunteers the skills they need to serve their peers. These volunteers are thus exposed to a professional career field, and if they are interested, they can get additional training to become paraprofessional staff members. Special structured workshops provide counseling and interviewing skills to both the volunteers and other campus and community groups which request such training.

(5) The research and evaluation team assesses the campus environment (by "ecomapping") to identify mismatches between students and their environment. The resulting data are fed back into

the campus community to initiate interventions that increase congruence. Subunits, such as residence halls, are also examined systematically when the staff requests help in enhancing the quality of student life. As evaluators, the team members consult with planners to develop and implement new programs and improve existing ones. They apply a systematic model of program initiation, implementation, and evaluation to all student development projects on the campus.

Strategies. Instruction, consultation, and milieu management are the three types of change strategies used. Members of the UCC staff lead groups that help the student function as a learner, as a service-giver, as a partner, as a member of a living community, as a woman or a man, as a worker, and in other roles. Various educational media such as audiotapes, videotapes, simulation games, and related materials and techniques are used whenever appropriate. Supervisory and consultative instructional techniques are utilized both with students and with others throughout the university community. The staff emphasizes teaching faculty members and students how to use group processes. The broad variety of consultation strategies has already been described. In general, the UCC acts as a consultation agency for the whole university, responding upon request. The milieu management strategies include several efforts that have also been mentioned—campus ecomapping, direct work with the residence communities, and establishment of a crisis/information-calling center. At all times, the UCC staff tries to collaborate with the faculty and other campus agencies to establish a university environment which is student-centered and in which all participants seek to respond to student needs.

Discussion. The UCC approach contains many elements of the proposed student development model. Goal setting, for instance, is evident in the collaboration between each student who applies for help and a student development educator (counselor) who helps the student decide what his or her needs are and what special programs will give most assistance in reaching those goals. Assessment is made with both formal standardized tests and informal self-evaluation efforts. In addition, the UCC completes periodic environment assessment projects, as mentioned above.

Integrating Programs

The three strategies for development—instruction, consultation, and milieu management—are reasonably well developed within the program. The career development modules help students explore various educational plans and establish realistic career goals. Clarification of work values, learning to make decisions, and research on occupations are all part of this instructional approach to career development. Likewise, formal teaching methods are used in the life planning workshops, the people-to-people program, and the student-couples seminars, as well as in the work of the behavior therapy teams. Since the UCC is the heart of this student development effort, consultation occurs most frequently in individual and group counseling. But in addition, staff members with expertise in organizational development, program development, and systems theory and training are available to students, staff members, and teachers to help them identify procedures which can enhance the educational experience and to locate stresses in the academic environment which detract from student development. Direct milieu management is the least emphasized activity in the UCC program. Probably the most noteworthy activity is the volunteer training project, which provides several benefits. The RoadHouse crisis center staffed by the volunteers gives emergency aid to both the campus and the local community, encouraging good mental health in these environments. And by having opportunities to become service-givers, students not only acquire useful skills and gain insight into a possible career but develop their sense of social responsibility.

Evaluation, the final component of the student development model, is well designed in the UCC program. The research and evaluation team works with all of the subprograms throughout their various stages, determining their impact on participants and thus ensuring effective service. The systematic approach to program initiation, implementation, and evaluation provides a solid basis for judging current programs and guiding the development of new ones.

PROGRAM TWO

In some cases an institution may base its mission on the premise that it should give students both a theoretical and practical frame-

175

work for integrating their college experience. Such is the view of Oakton Community College in Morton Grove, Illinois, which has devised a Comprehensive Community College Student Development Program. It is concerned with students before they enter, during their course of study, and after they leave the institution. And the variety of students it hopes to reach is equally wide: young adults, women returning to school, fully employed part-time evening students, and senior citizens.

Rationale. Since Oakton itself is constructed on a student development model, this particular program has the broad purposes one expects. As it seeks to serve a diverse group of students over a long period, it meets them in and out of the classroom and touches on many developmental needs, including the academic, the social, the personal, and the vocational.

Goals. (1) To help students see themselves as always being in the process of development, always changing and growing. (2) To show students that the various aspects of their lives are interrelated and integrated rather than fragmented. (3) To expose students to developmental stimuli throughout their college experience, both within and outside the formal classroom. (4) To encounter students at whatever developmental point they may be and promote further change and growth.

Structure. The Office of Student Development, directed by the vice president for student development, is responsible for implementing these goals throughout the college. The staff comprises full-time faculty members and professional administrators, including representatives from the Admission and Records Office, the Athletics Department, the Student Activities Office, and the women's programs. Twelve of these people, who are designated the student development faculty, do educational, vocational, and personal counseling in addition to teaching. They are divided among the college's four learning clusters (minicolleges), and each subgroup of three is responsible to the dean of one cluster (for their teaching and other "academic" tasks). They work directly with the faculty and students of their cluster and have offices adjoining their colleagues. Thus, counseling services are both decentralized—in that student development faculty members are located in each of the college buildings—and integrated, since counselors are found in each cluster complex along with other faculty members.

Specific Programs and Objectives. One of the first programs students engage in is the Life and Career Planning Workshop, which gives all entrants opportunities to explore their life goals, vocational aims, and program choices so that they will be better able to select the courses that are right for them. The Psychology of Personal Growth focuses on emotional or affective development. Combining humanistic psychology, group dynamics, and theories of human development, it helps individuals build on their strengths, examine their values, and work toward achieving their goals. The tandem courses (described in Chapter Four) give students both cognitive and affective learning experiences in multidisciplinary classes under the guidance of a teaching team. They facilitate an understanding of how self and subject matter are related. In the women's programs, participants work on those developmental tasks particularly associated with being a female, whether they are just entering adulthood or are in a mature stage. The program especially helps women returning to school make the needed adjustments to be successful in college. The Success Seminar Project gives students in the developmental reading program opportunities to improve their self-image through experiencing success within a group setting, as well as to develop study skills. Various informal educational programs, such as the human sexuality seminars, offer students opportunities to develop in personal ways not directly related to their formal education.

Faculty members also take part in programs to improve their instruction methods and learn ways of creating a sense of group or community within a given class. Student development educators who are skilled at managing group processes are available to work with teachers in the classroom, too. Those instructors who also function as academic advisors are given some assistance in learning to work sensitively with students as mentors and role models.

Both individual and group counseling are available to students who need help with personal, vocational, or academic concerns. The student development faculty holds office hours at night so

177

that part-time and evening students can obtain counseling and advisement as well. The testing program is an important adjunct to counseling and advising. All incoming students are tested in mathematics, writing, and reading. And vocational interest and personality inventories are available for use by students who wish to examine these aspects of their development.

Strategies. Instruction by the student development faculty is an element in several of the programs described above: the Psychology of Personal Growth; the tandem courses, in which a student development faculty member is half of the teaching team; the success seminars, taught in conjunction with the developmental reading program; and the informal, noncredit education programs. In general, the student development faculty is striving to incorporate the humanistic, developmental approach in all parts of the curriculum, both formal and informal.

Members of this special subfaculty also act as consultants to a variety of programs—faculty development, to build instructional and advisory skills; student leadership development; peer advisor training; individual and group counseling; career development; and the senior citizens' and women's programs. Strategies for managing the environment have included: establishing classroom climates conducive to personal development as well as cognitive growth; creating four learning clusters with differing characteristics; and organizing the learning milieu so that students are exposed to numerous educational stimuli and opportunities for involvement. Among the latter are the Semester for Self-Directed Study, the Green Turnip (Academic) Survival Program, the Values Program, American Studies, Focus: Chicago, the human sexuality seminars, the leadership training program, the Life and Career Planning Workshop, and the peer advisor program. Another strategy, mentioned earlier, is placing the student development faculty offices in many accessible locations.

Discussion. The several elements of the proposed student development approach have been integrated in the Oakton program. Goal setting occurs in the classroom and among staff and faculty members who are developing job descriptions and planning their educational activities. Assessment has both academic and personal

178

dimensions. In addition to the tests and inventories cited above, the program uses self-report instruments with students in the various programs, and the student development faculty makes systematic observations of students throughout the campus community.

Although instruction is the primary developmental strategy used, both consultation and milieu management strategies are evident. The student development faculty works with academic faculty members in both formal and informal settings. For instance, they collaborated on creating the academic advisement system which is guided primarily by the student development educators.

Important aspects of the comprehensive environmental management plan are the four learning clusters which are designed to respond to the needs of different students. Variety and balance are the bases for assigning faculty members and students to the learning clusters, not homogeneity. Each cluster contains a balance of academic disciplines as well as learning resource faculty, student development faculty, and vocational-technical faculty. For example, one cluster at Oakton might have a business instructor; from three to five communications instructors; one foreign language instructor; from one to three instructors in humanities; from three to six mathematics and science faculty members; and from two to four social science teachers. Each learning cluster constitutes a small, nondepartmental "inner college"; its unifying principle is the limitation of group size in order to maintain "recognizability." The learning clusters offer students both cognitive and social-affective values in that they have opportunities to relate to peers and to faculty and staff members in an intimate way more suited to meeting their individual needs (Koehnline, 1975).

Another valuable effort is the peer advisor program, which employs nine students who advise other students. These advisors, both trained and supervised by the student development faculty, help to humanize the educational experience of the whole student body.

Regular evaluation procedures involve both students and faculty. Students rate the teachers and content of each program in which they participate. And the student development faculty and other staff members make similar program evaluations throughout

179

the year. The office of the vice president for student development completes an annual report that integrates all of these evaluations, identifying present program strengths and weaknesses and suggesting appropriate future directions. Each member of the student development faculty—and every other teacher as well—is formally evaluated once a year by the dean of his or her learning cluster, and in the case of the student development faculty, by the vice president for student development. Both instructional effectiveness (as measured by formal student evaluations) and institutional effectiveness (projects, committee work, and so on) are assessed. The ongoing Student Development Inservice Training Program responds to the staff development needs that are identified.

PROGRAM THREE

A few postsecondary institutions have tried to implant the human development concept even more deeply in their environment. Although they still give primary attention to students, they are also concerned with the continued development of the faculty and the administrative staff. In this milieu, every inhabitant and every facility is part of the total program. The main barrier to this comprehensive plan is the limited amount of time that all the participants can devote to discussion and implementation. Obviously, achieving this goal is no simple matter, nor can it be accomplished in a short time. The commitment needs to be total, but the potential rewards are great.

One institution that is striving to create this type of institutional environment is Azusa Pacific College in California. Its Small College Model for Development of the Whole Person, coordinated by the Department of Student Development, is designed primarily for undergraduates and graduate students, secondarily for members of the faculty, staff, and administration.

Rationale. Student life at Azusa is based on the "whole person" concept: the student is not only an intellectual being, but a spiritual, emotional, and social being as well. The Department of Student Development is committed to giving students opportunities to develop all these aspects of their nature so that during their college experience they will have a chance to become what they have been created to be. Essentially, student life proceeds in an environment that incorporates a variety of structured and unstructured means to learning and that offers a time and a place where one can discover personal potential and have one's self-worth reinforced while developing a fulfilling philosophy of life.

Goals. (1) To provide opportunities for growth in a Christian environment designed to facilitate the realization and acquisition of academic, physical, and social abilities, autonomy and corporateness; to clarify individual values and direction; and to help students establish personal integrity and faith. (2) To give special attention to particular groups of students—such as residents, off-campus students, terminating students, veterans, minority students, and those with definable needs, such as academic skills, emotional management, and career education.

Structure. The Department of Student Development, under the leadership of the dean of student development and the department chairperson, is directly responsible for developing and implementing specific programs. Administrators and members of the faculty and staff serve first as models and second as resources. The student works with both the professional staff and other students in exploring and learning from what the college offers. The student development professionals, as well as all other college employees, facilitate the learning process, enabling each student to use the available resources to enhance his or her personal development. In addition, graduate student interns, who are specializing in student development programming, work in all parts of the program.

Specific Programs and Objectives. The Personal and Career Counseling Resource Center is the base of operations. It offers self-help programs in such areas as academic skills and career exploration. It also provides standardized testing for students as a prelude to counseling. Students can go there to get help with their personal and vocational problems, to take noncredit developmental seminars, and to participate in structured, growth-promoting experiences. The Center also coordinates several "theme activities," such as Career Emphasis Week.

A variety of personal development courses are offered. A

Leadership, Management, and Student Developmental Theory course is available and required for all undergraduates applying for positions as peer counselors, admissions interns, and student body officers. An inservice Personal Functioning and Interpersonal Relations Seminar is also required for all peer counselors. A graduate course on the American College Student using Chickering's seven vectors of development (1969) is offered as part of the Student Development Internship Program. A four-month independent study course based on the Australian aboriginal rite of passage, "The Walkabout," allows students to relate personal goals to the principles of adventure, creativity, service to others, logical inquiry, and celebration. An eight-day Wilderness Stress Program is available to students wishing to develop self-sufficiency and confidence. This course is also a major element in the training of the residence hall staff. Other developmental seminars and opportunities for growth are available to students, individually or in groups, without academic credit.

As part of the Faculty Development Program, task forces comprising members of the faculty, college staff, administration, and student development staff are established to deal with special institutional issues and concerns. Faculty forums give teachers current information on matters affecting students. And the Department of Student Development provides consultation services to individual faculty members and academic programs on request.

Student groups with special needs have programs designed just for them. For instance, resident students may choose a developmental or educational theme that will be emphasized in their living area. And students can create their own special-interest class or outdoor adventure program. Students also have opportunities to plan and implement campuswide "interest weeks."

Azusa Pacific has an assessment program called the Student-Centered Management Information System (SCMIS). An instrument administered to all incoming students during orientation provides a comprehensive and constantly updated profile of the student body's personal characteristic and needs. The System also surveys students' social interests and academic activities, their views on campus morale, faculty functioning, and residence life, and their religious and other personal experiences. The results, which are made available to all members of the campus community, allow student development planners to respond systematically to the current needs of students rather than guess what they require.

Strategies. Both formal and informal development instruction is an integral part of the curriculum. The personal development courses described earlier are regularly offered for credit, and optional independent study opportunities are available, too. Student paraprofessionals and student leaders are required to take some of these classes as part of their training. The student development faculty also provides tutorial programs, teaches students special skills—how to study and how to decide on a career, for example—and offers various other seminars on subjects that interest students. They "instruct" their colleagues, as well, by disseminating information on students via the faculty forums. By giving credit for developmental courses, the college validates its position that personal growth is valued and deserving of formal recognition.

The consultation strategies of the student development department include individual and group work with students who want to deal with such concerns as emotional problems, career exploration, and academic difficulties. These faculty members also consult with students in the peer counseling program, the Associated Student Body Administrative Council, the residence hall living area councils, and the Koinonia faith development groups. They play a guidance role in the ongoing faculty development program, and they form consultation teams that help to deal with campus issues.

The milieu is managed in several ways, most of which have been mentioned under other headings. Designing residence halls to respond to the needs of students at different developmental levels is one management strategy. Another is the Experimental College (part of the Campus Center), where students can create their own classes. The Personal and Career Counseling Resource Center is an essential element in the environmental management program, too.

Discussion. The elements of the proposed student development model are clearly manifested in the Azusa Pacific program.

Goal setting occurs many times during the students' college experience. The extent and intensity of each student's involvement in personal development activity are left to him or her to determine. However, because the whole institution is focused on human development, all students become involved to some degree. Students are encouraged to establish tangible objectives for their development when they enter the institution as well as at the beginning of each semester and each course. Through this process of systematic advisement and reinforcement, students learn to set goals and objectives as a normal part of their education.

The primary assessment tool, the SCMIS, is essentially broad and environmental. More personal assessment instruments include a self-monitoring developmental guide and check sheet which each resident student can use to help choose a living environment that will do the most to meet his or her personal needs. By using this procedure, the student learns how to use self-assessment as a guide to goal achievement and advanced personal development. Standardized measurements are also available for those who wish to appraise their academic achievement, their personal interests, their career objectives, their personality, and other aspects of self.

Most of the change strategies used have been described above. As noted, developmental instruction is considered important and is offered through various means, such as the Experimental College, the Personal and Career Counseling Resource Center, and the college convocation program. A valuable kind of consultation is the training and supervision of students who act as peer advisors and paraprofessionals. This program does a great deal to implement the personal development model throughout the campus. Another noteworthy strategy involves graduate students who are seeking an M.A. in Social Science with an emphasis in student development—perhaps the only program currently being offered by a small Christian college to prepare student development professionals in higher education. The graduate students function as interns and consultants to undergraduates. Perhaps the most unusual environmental management strategy is giving resident students an opportunity to select a personal development theme for their living units. The freedom offered by the Experimental College also makes it possible for the individual student to identify and participate with others who wish to achieve similar personal goals. Other, more traditional but still worthwhile techniques include the campus "interest week" programs, on such topics as developing a meaningful religious faith or examining the concerns of professional women, and the self-help programs available through the Resource Center.

Like the assessment procedures, the program evaluation methods are quite sophisticated. Azusa Pacific uses the Results Systems Management Model developed by Keirsey and Bates (1972), in which every program goal is based on a need assessment, stated as a result for which one is willing to be held accountable, explicitly expressed in outcome statements to which all parties agree, and articulated so that everyone knows the criteria for success. And each activity is monitored and appraised by an objective manager. This systematic approach allows the evaluator to judge various programs in similar ways so that valid comparisons can be made among them. This RSM approach is also used to guide individual development. For example, student development staff members may draw up with an individual student a personal Results System Management Contract designed to help overcome barriers to effective functioning within the residence community. Obviously, such procedures, which must be built in from the beginning rather than added as an after thought, are fully compatible with the student development model being proposed.

CREATING DEVELOPMENTAL PROGRAMS

Student developmental programs can be created and integrated in the campus environment in many ways. Identifying the kinds of developmental tasks students need to undertake and responding to them with purposeful programs are important skills for student affairs professionals to possess. The following steps show how one might approach such programming using the functions and abilities previously outlined.

Developmental Task. Develop assertiveness.

185

Outcome Objective. Develop the eye contact, body postures, facial expressions, voice tone, and correct manner of expressing content that characterize an assertive act.

Assessment. (1) Behavioral observation: the staff member presents stimulus statements to students, then assesses their assertive, aggressive, and nonassertive responses. (2) Instruments: the staff member administers the Assertiveness Inventory and the Edwards Personal Preference Schedule. (3) Self-report: the student reports behaving in nonassertive ways.

Change Strategies. (1) *Milieu Management:* the staff person offers those desiring more assertive behavior a place to live together with someone who has a higher level of assertive skills; creates situations in which they will have to demonstrate assertive behavior; presents a workshop for faculty members with the goal of teaching them how to attend and respond to assertive behavior in the classroom. (2) *Consultation:* the staff member responds to requests of individuals or groups and gives information on assertive behavior versus aggressive behavior; provides opportunities for modeling assertive behavior with feedback; discusses emotional blocks to assertive behavior and examines reasons for and possible consequences of such behavior. (3) *Instruction:* the educator offers a course in assertiveness training that includes the elimination of self-defeating behavior; *Your Perfect Right* is used as a textbook.

Program Evaluation. Students engage in simulated roleplaying situations that demand assertive behavior; the educator rates their performance in terms of eye contact, posture, voice tone, and content of presentation; staff member seeks environment feedback.

Developmental Task. Develop listening skills.

Outcome objective. Develop perception and attending behavior, be able to hear both content and affective (nonverbal) components of communication.

Assessment. (1) Behavioral observation: The educator observes student interaction in both group and individual situations; presents stimulus statements (in a simulated setting), then assesses the ability of the student to pick up on content and affect, assesses the level of attending behavior, and assesses the degree of perception.

(2) Instrumentation: the staff member measures the ability of the student to reflect accurately the content and affective components of statements by using a Carkhuff-type rating scale; uses independent raters. (3) Self-report: the student reports expressing dissatisfactions in interactions with others.

Change Strategies. (1) *Milieu Management:* the educator offers staff development programs for faculty and staff members to improve their listening skills in working with students and others; the staff member evaluates their behavior by observing it or by rating it in a simulated setting. (2) *Consultation:* the educator advises individuals or groups on ways of practicing better listening behavior; discusses attitudes and feelings that interfere with listening; evaluates by getting feedback from the groups and individuals being advised; observes their behavior. (3) *Instruction:* the educator offers a course or structured experience or workshop that includes information, modeling, practice, and feedback about the listening behavior of participants; evaluates by observing their behavior or using self-ratings and peer ratings; makes tapes for independent raters' use.

THE FUTURE OF STUDENT DEVELOPMENT

The three extended examples presented in this chapter, as well as the many shorter descriptions scattered throughout the book, have demonstrated the complexities of organizing and implementing an integrated student development program. Yet despite the obstacles, we must continue to aim high. Although individual programs and activities undertaken by subunits of the institution are certainly valuable, we should strive for the broadest and deepest manifestion we can achieve. This book has offered no panaceas; in fact, the hard work is really just beginning. Model building is fun and useful, but it is not more than a first step. Nevertheless, it is hoped that the philosophy and processes portrayed here will spur those who find them sound and agreeable to test them in their own institutions. Only by trying them out in the field will we ultimately be able to determine whether this approach is valid for the great variety of postsecondary institutions in this country and beyond.

Before such field testing can be done on a broad scale, however, much more attention should be given to finding the best organizational structure and methods for implementing the model. Equally important is the preservice and inservice training of those who will carry out these programs. Until there are professionally educated individuals to undertake the specific tasks and strategies called for, full testing or implementation will be impossible. The future requires a concerted effort to find practical preparation methods and materials. Our budding professionals and paraprofessionals, as well as those already working in student affairs, are being asked to handle many complex functions—goal setting, assessment, evaluation, instruction, consultation, and milieu management—and they will need help and support to do so.

Other important work that should increase in the future is gathering and disseminating information and materials related to the student development approach. Finding ways to share what is going on among professionals so that they can learn from one another and to distribute relevant data and recommendations is essential. This book is only one contribution to that effort. There is also a continuing need to identify and assist institutions that are attempting to implement integrated programs, as well as to encourage other colleges to take the plunge.

So there is much to be done as higher education professionals move toward the goal of student development. Now we must marshal our resources and collaborate on the hard work that lies ahead. It is hoped that you and your colleagues will join in this adventure in developing whole human beings in tomorrow's higher education.

Appendix

꙳꙳꙳꙳꙳꙳꙳꙳

Program Examples
and Contact Persons

GOAL SETTING

*Risking Change: Goal Setting for My Personal and Professional Development, State University College at Buffalo
  William F. Sturner
  Vice President for Academic Affairs
  State University College at Buffalo
  1300 Elmwood Avenue
  Buffalo, New York 14222

* An asterisk indicates those examples discussed in the book.

189

Appendix

*Ideas—Individual Development: Encounter with the Arts and Sciences, Austin College
>Howard A. Starr
>Associate Dean
>Professor of Psychology and Education
>Austin College
>Sherman, Texas 75090

*A Program for the Development and Training of Student Leaders, Wesleyan College
>Joyce R. Schafer
>Dean of Student Affairs
>Wesleyan College
>Macon, Georgia 31201

Semester Goals Project, Iona College
>Frederick R. Brodzinski
>Director of Residence
>Iona College—Rice Hall
>New Rochelle, N.Y. 10801

ASSESSMENT

*Implementing a Model Individual Planning Program, Mara Institute of Technology
>Tom Waters, Consultant
>Counselling Unit
>Mara Institute of Technology
>Shah Alam
>Telangor, Malaysia

*The Phone Survey: An Environment Assessment Technique, Illinois State University
>Robert K. Conyne
>512 DeGarmo Hall
>Illinois State University
>Normal, Illinois 61761

Appendix

*An Environmental Assessment Inventory for Counseling Center Para-
professional Students, Illinois State University
> Robert K. Conyne
> 512 DeGarmo Hall
> Illinois State University
> Normal, Illinois 61761

*The Student Self-Assessment Program, El Centro College
> Don Creamer
> Dean of Students
> El Centro College
> Main and Lamar Streets
> Dallas, Texas 75202

INSTRUCTION

*Student Development in the Classroom: The Tandem Approach,
Oakton Community College
> Steven R. Helfgot
> Assistant Professor of Student Development
> Oakton Community College
> 6900 North Nagle Avenue
> Morton Grove, Illinois 60053

*The Human Development Curriculum, El Centro College
> Don Creamer
> Dean of Students
> and Dr. Jerry Wesson
> Division Chairman of Human Development
> El Centro College
> Main and Lamar Streets
> Dallas, Texas 75202

*The Awareness Series: A Program of Personal and Organizational
Development, Virginia Commonwealth University
> Alfred T. Matthews
> Dean of Student Life

Appendix

Virginia Commonwealth University
901 West Franklin Street
Richmond, Virginia 23284

*Self and the Campus Society, The University of Texas at Austin
Margaret Berry
Director of Developmental Programs
Office of Vice President for Student Affairs
The University of Texas at Austin
Austin, Texas 78712

Proficiency Credit Program, William Rainey Harper College
Gary Rankin
Dean of Student Services
William Rainey Harper College
Palatine, Illinois 60067

SUCCESS: Students under Constant Challenge for Educational Success, Hillsborough Community College
Sister Rosanne Jones
Coordinator of Human Development
Hillsborough Community College
P.O. Box 22127
Tampa, Florida 33622

Career Planning, Hostos Community College
Robert T. Tyler
Director
Cooperative Education
Eugenio Maria de Hostos Community College
of the City University of New York
475 Grand Concourse
Bronx, New York 10451

The Study of Blacks and Whites: Student Development in Intergroup Relations, Illinois State University
Robert K. Conyne
512 De Garmo Hall

Appendix

Student Counseling Center
Illinois State University
Normal, Illinois 61761

Life Planning: An Aid to the Advisory System, The University of Vermont
  Janet W. Forgays
  Counselor
  Counseling and Testing Center
  University of Vermont
  146 South Williams Street
  Burlington, Vermont 05401

CONSULTATION

*Peer Academic Advising Program, University of Georgia
  Kenneth L. Ender
  Student Development Specialist
  Franklin College of Arts and Sciences
  New College
  University of Georgia
  Athens, Georgia 30602

Small Group Leadership Workshop: A Professional Development Program, Illinois State University
  Lynn S. Rapin, Staff Counselor
  Student Counseling Center
  520 De Garmo Hall
  Illinois State University
  Normal, Illinois 61761

Academic Consultation Service, Howard University
  Howard N. Johnson
  University Counseling Service
  Howard University
  Washington, D.C. 20059

Appendix

*Faculty Mini-Workshops, Eastfield College
    Joe Tinnin
    Director of Counseling
    Eastfield College
    3737 Motley Drive
    Mesquite, Texas 75149

Learning Improving Program, Eastfield College
    Joe Tinnin
    Director of Counseling
    Eastfield College
    3737 Motley Drive
    Mesquite, Texas 75149

Faculty Advising Project, University of Nebraska at Lincoln
    Janet Krause
    Program Developer
    Counseling Center
    1316 Seaton Hall
    University of Nebraska at Lincoln
    Lincoln, Nebraska 68508

*Interpersonal Skills Workshop, Illinois State University
    R. James Clack
    Student Counseling Center
    Illinois State University
    Normal, Illinois 61761

*Faculty Development Workshop: Understanding the Campus Environment, University of Illinois
    Robert K. Conyne
    Coordinator of Consultation
    Student Counseling Center
    De Garmo 515
    Illinois State University
    Normal, Illinois 61761

Career Development Services for the Student Counseling Center, Illinois State University
    Donald J. Cochran

Appendix

Coordinator of Career Development
De Garmo Hall 511
Illinois State University
Normal, Illinois 61761

*Adventure Training for Resident Advisers, Auburn University, Auburn, Alabama
Charles C. Schroeder
Director, Men's Housing Magnolia Dormitories
Auburn University
Auburn, Alabama 36830

Academic Support Groups, Illinois State University
R. James Clack
Student Counseling Center
Illinois State University
Normal, Illinois 61761

Student Development Through Academic Advising, University of Maryland
Thomas J. Grites
Supervisor, Student Records and Advising Officer
College of Education
University of Maryland
College Park, Maryland 20742

Academic Advisement as Predicted by the California Psychological Inventory: Examination of the Effect of Pre-College Counseling and Group Counseling on Attrition
Edward P. Martinez
245 W. Loraine
Glendale, California 91202

Class Profile Analysis; Encounter with Eastfield; Senior College Transfer Guide; Field Trips as Growth Labs, Eastfield College
Joe Tinnin
Director of Counseling
Eastfield College
3737 Motley Drive
Mesquite, Texas 75149

Appendix

Behavioral Management of Overeating, Illinois State University
Alan R. Sodetz
Staff Counselor
Student Counselor Service
De Garmo Hall
Illinois State University
Normal, Illinois 61761

*Career Action Commission, The University of Nebraska at Lincoln
Janet Krause
Acting Chairperson of Career Action Commission
1316 Seaton Hall
University of Nebraska at Lincoln
Lincoln, Nebraska 68508

Faculty Associates Program, Oklahoma State University
W. Lynn Jackson
Director
Office of Single Student Housing Program Development
Oklahoma State University
354 Student Union
Stillwater, Oklahoma 74074

Special Services Program, Oklahoma State University
Terry H. Henderson
Coordinator, Special Services
Oklahoma State University
Stillwater, Oklahoma 74074

A Formula for Program Success: Students and Organization and Creativity, Oklahoma State University
Jan M. Carlson
Director of Student Activities
Oklahoma State University
Stillwater, Oklahoma 74074
(Program developed by:
Jo F. Dorris
Associate Dean)

Fuzzies Program: An Outreach Program for the Counseling Service, University of Oklahoma

Appendix

Rex T. Finnegan
Director of University Counseling Services
Oklahoma State University
Stillwater, Oklahoma 74074

*Student Development Laboratory, University of Georgia
Theodore K. Miller
Director, Student Development Laboratory
408 Aderhold Hall
University of Georgia
Athens, Georgia 30602

MILIEU MANAGEMENT

*Project Greek, Iowa State University
Allen L. Peterson
Program Advisor, Greek Affairs
237 Student Health Services
Iowa State University
Ames, Iowa 50010

*Multi-Ethnic Program, University of California at Davis
Karen Lee Hawkins
Assistant Director of Housing
Segundo Annex, Room 111
Housing Business Office
University of California
Davis, California 95616

*A Student Development Model at a Liberal Arts College, Hood College
Janet A. Carl
Director of Student Development
Hood College
Frederick, Maryland 21701

Student Development Program in the University Division of General Studies, Bowling Green State University
Diane DeVestern
Modular Achievement Program
26 Shatzel Hall

Bowling Green State University
Bowling Green, Ohio 43403

*Territoriality and the Group System: New Strategies for Structuring Residential Environments, Auburn University
    Charles C. Schroeder
    Director, Men's Housing
    Magnolia Dormitories
    Auburn University
    Auburn, Alabama 36830

*The Educational Development Group Enrichment (EDGE) Program: A Comprehensive Model for Student Development in College and University Residence Halls, Bowling Green State University
    Gregory Bliming
    Director, Anderson Hall
    Bowling Green State University
    Bowling Green, Ohio 43403

*Competence-Based Learning, Alverno College
    Alverno College
    3401 South 39th Street
    Milwaukee, Wisconsin 53215

Freshman Human Services, The University of Nebraska at Lincoln
    Vernon Williams
    Director, Counseling Center
    1316 Seaton Hall
    University of Nebraska
    Lincoln, Nebraska 68508

EVALUATION

*Growth Strategies for a Developmental Staff Evaluation Program, University of Minnesota, Duluth
    Tom Thielen
    Vice Provost for Student Affairs
    University of Minnesota, Duluth
    Duluth, Minnesota, 55802

Appendix

*Colleague Evaluation in the Counseling Center, El Centro College
> Don Creamer
> Dean of Students
> El Centro College
> Main and Lamar Streets
> Dallas, Texas 75202

Developing a Model for Assessment of Student Personnel Outcomes, William Rainey Harper College
> Gary E. Rankin
> Dean of Student Services
> William Rainey Harper College
> Palatine, Illinois 60067

Evaluation Procedures for Freshman Programs and Services, Oklahoma State University
> Robert G. Schmalfeld
> Dean of Student Services
> Oklahoma State University
> Stillwater, Oklahoma 74074

ORGANIZATION

*SASCH: Student Activities, Student Center, and Housing, Trenton State College
> William M. Klepper
> Director, Group Student Development Services,
> Trenton State College
> Trenton, New Jersey 08625

The 4 x 4 Model for Student Development, University of Maryland
> Thomas J. Grites
> Supervisor, Student Records and Advising Office
> College of Education
> University of Maryland
> College Park, Maryland 20742

The Organizational Structure of Student Affairs, Oklahoma State University
> Robert G. Schmalfeld

199

Appendix

Dean of Student Affairs
Oklahoma State University
Stillwater, Oklahoma 74074

INTEGRATED PROGRAMS

*A Comprehensive Community College Student Development Program,
Oakton Community College
  John P. Donohue
  Vice President for Student Development,
  Oakton Community College
  7900 North Nagle
  Morton Grove, Illinois 60053

*An Integrated Student Development Approach, Azusa Pacific College
  Andrea C. McAleenan
  Chairperson, Department of Student Development,
  Azusa, California 91702

*The University Counseling Center, Colorado State University
  James C. Hurst
  Director, Counseling Center
  Colorado State University
  Fort Collins, Colorado 80523

Community-Based Student Services, Kellogg Community College
  Hans A. Andrews
  Kellogg Community College
  450 North Avenue
  Battle Creek, Michigan 49016

Complementary Education: A Concept for the Enrichment of Learning
and the Development of Students, Faculty, and Staff, Rochester Institute of Technology

  Fred W. Smith
  Vice President for Student Affairs and
  Dean of Complementary Education
  Division of Student Affairs
  Rochester Institute of Technology
  Rochester, New York 14623

References

ALVERNO COLLEGE. "Competence-Based Learning at Alverno College." Milwaukee, 1975.

American College Personnel Association, Tomorrow's Higher Education Project, T. K. Miller, (Chmn.) "A Student Development Model for Student Affairs in Tomorrow's Higher Education." *Journal of College Student Personnel,* 1975, *16,* 334–341.

AMERICAN COLLEGE TESTING PROGRAM. *Career Planning Program,* Rev. Iowa City, 1976.

ANASTASI, A. *Psychological Testing.* 3rd ed. New York: Macmillan, 1968.

ANDERSON, S. B., BALL, S., MURPHY, R. T., and ASSOCIATES. *Encyclopedia of Educational Evaluation.* San Francisco: Jossey-Bass, 1975.

ASTIN, A. W. *The College Environment.* Washington: American Council on Education, 1968.

ASTIN, A. W. *Manual for the Inventory of College Activities.* Minneapolis: National Computer Systems, 1971.

ASTIN, A. W., and HOLLAND, J. L. "The Environmental Assessment Tech-

References

niques: A Way to Measure College Environments." *Journal of Educational Psychology,* 1961, *52,* 308–316.

AULEPP, L., and DELWORTH, U. *Training Manual for an Ecosystem Model: Assisting and Designing Campus Environments.* Boulder: Western Interstate Commission for Higher Education, 1976.

BANGHART, F. *Education System Analysis.* London: Macmillan, 1969.

BANK, A. "Techniques for Analyzing Needs." In R. Loring (Ed.), *Sound of Change.* Los Angeles: University of California at Los Angeles, 1974.

BANKS, W., and MARTENS, K. "Counseling: The Reactionary Profession." *Personnel and Guidance Journal,* 1972, *51,* 457–462.

BANNING, J. H., and KAISER, L. "An Ecological Perspective and Model for Campus Design." *Personnel and Guidance Journal,* 1974, *52,* 370–375.

BARBER, T. X., and OTHERS (Eds.) *Biofeedback and Self-Control.* Chicago: Aldine-Atherton, 1971.

BARCLAY, J. R. *Testing for Higher Education: Cultural Perspective and Future Focus.* Washington: American College Personnel Association, 1965.

BARKER, R. G. *Ecological Psychology: Concepts and Methods for Studying the Environment of Human Behavior.* Stanford: Stanford University Press, 1968.

BENNIS, W. G. "A Typology of Change Processes." In W. C. Bennis, K. D. Benne, and R. Chin (Eds.), *The Planning of Change.* New York: Holt, Rinehart, and Winston, 1969.

BENNIS, W. G., BENNE, K. D., and CHIN, R. (Eds.) *The Planning of Change: Readings in the Applied Bebavioral Sciences.* 2nd ed. New York: Holt, Rinehart, and Winston, 1969.

BLOCHER, D. H. *Developmental Counseling.* New York: Ronald, 1966.

BLOCHER, D. H. "Toward an Ecology of Student Development." *Personnel and Guidance Journal,* 1974, *52,* 360–365.

BLOCHER, D. H. "A Systematic Eclectic Approach to Consultation." In C. A. Parker (Ed.), *Psychological Consultation: Helping Teachers Meet Special Needs.* Minneapolis: University of Minnesota, 1975.

BLOOM, B. S. (Ed.), *Taxonomy of Educational Objectives, Handbook I: Cognitive Development.* New York: McKay, 1956.

BLOOM, B. S., HASTINGS, J. T., and MADEUS, G. F. *Handbook on Forma-*

References

tive and Summative Evaluation of Student Learning. New York: McGraw-Hill, 1971.

BLOS, P. *The Adolescent Personality: A Study of Individual Behavior.* New York: Appleton-Century, 1941.

BOWERS, C. A. "Accountability from a Humanist Point of View." In F. J. Sciara and R. K. Jantz (Eds.), *Accountability in American Education.* Boston: Allyn and Bacon, 1972.

BRADFORD, L. P. "The Teaching-Learning Transaction." *Adult Education,* 1958, *8,* 135–145.

BROWN, G. I. *Human Teaching for Human Learning: An Introduction to Confluent Education.* New York: Viking, 1970.

BROWN, R. D. *Student Development in Tomorrow's Higher Education: A Return to the Academy.* Student Personnel Series No. 16. Washington: American College Personnel Association, 1972.

BROWN, R. D., and CITRIN, R. S. *Implications of the Ying-Yang Theory of Student Development for Assessment: A Student Development Transcript.* A paper read at the American College Personnel Association Convention, Atlanta, Georgia, March 7, 1975.

BRUNER, J. S. "The Process of Education Revisited." *Phi Delta Kappan,* Sept. 1971, 18–21.

BURCK, H. D., and PETERSON, G. W. "Needed: More Evaluation, Not Research." *Personnel and Guidance Journal,* 1975, *53,* 563–569.

CAMPBELL, D. R., and HOLLAND, J. L. "A Merger in Vocational Research: Applying Holland's Theory to Strong's Data." *Journal of Vocational Behavior,* 1972, *2,* 353–376.

CAPLAN, G. *The Theory and Practice of Mental Health Consultation.* New York: Basic Books, 1970.

CHANDLER, E. M. "Student Affairs Administration in Transition." *Journal of College Student Personnel,* 1973, *14,* 292–398.

"Change in Liberal Education: A Prospectus." Washington: Association of American Colleges, 1974.

CHICKERING, A. W. *Education and Identity.* San Francisco: Jossey-Bass, 1969.

CLACK, R., and CONYNE, R. "Interpersonal Skills Scale." Unpublished document, Illinois State University, 1973.

CLARK, B. R., and TROW, M. "The Organizational Context." In I. M. Newcomb and E. K. Wilson (Eds.), *College Peer Groups: Problems and Prospects for Research.* Chicago: Aldine, 1966.

References

COHEN, B. D., and MARCH, J. G. *Leadership and Ambiguity.* New York: McGraw-Hill, 1974.

COHEN, R. D. *Students and Colleges: Need-Press Dimensions for the Development of a Common Framework for Characterizing Students and Colleges.* (Ed. 01 1083) Washington: U.S. Office of Education, 1966.

COHEN, S., and HERSH, R. "Behaviorism and Humanism: A Synthesis for Teachers." *Journal of Teacher Education,* 1972, *23,* 172–176.

COLEMAN, J. *The Adolescent Society.* New York: Free Press, 1963.

COLORADO STATE UNIVERSITY. *University Counseling Center.* Ft. Collins, 1975.

COMBS, A. W., AVILA, D. C., and PURKEY, W. W. *Helping Relationships.* Boston: Allyn and Bacon, 1971.

CONYNE, R. K. "Environmental Assessment: Mapping for Counselor Action." *Personnel and Guidance Journal,* 1975, *54,* 151–154.

CONYNE, R. K., and COCHRAN, D. J. "Academia and Career Development Toward Integration." *Personnel and Guidance Journal,* 1973, *52,* 217–223.

COONS, F. W. "The Developmental Tasks of College Students." in S. C. Feinstein, P. L. Glovacchini, and A. A. Miller (Eds.), *Adolescent Psychiatry: Developmental and Clinical Studies.* Vol. 1. New York: Basic Books, 1971.

COWLEY, W. H. "Reflections of a Troublesome But Hopeful Rip Van Winkle." *Journal of College Student Personnel,* 1964, *6,* 66–73.

COYLE, T. H. "Students Expect Teachers To Do More Than Teach." *Journal of College Student Personnel,* 1971, *12,* 58–61.

CRAIG, R. "Lawrence Kohlberg and Moral Development: Some Reflections." *Educational Theory,* 1974, *24,* 121–129.

CREAMER, D. "Implementing Student Development." Paper Presented at the American College Personnel Association Convention, Atlanta, March 1975.

CROOKSTON, B. B. "A Developmental View of Academic Advising as Teaching." *Journal of College Student Personnel,* 1972a, *13,* 12–17.

CROOKSTON, B. B. "An Organization Model for Student Development." *NASPA Journal,* 1972b, *10,* 3–13.

CROOKSTON, B. B. "Education for Human Development." In C. F. Warnath and Associates, *New Directions for College Counselors.* San Francisco: Jossey-Bass, 1973.

References

CROOKSTON, B. B. "A Design for an Intentional Democratic Community." In D. A. DeCoster and P. Mable (Eds.), *Student Development and Education in College Residence Halls.* Washington: American College Personnel Association, 1974.

CROOKSTON, B. B. "Student Personnel: All Hail and Farewell!" *Personnel and Guidance Journal,* 1976, *55* 26–29.

CROOKSTON, B. B. "Milieu Management: An Emerging Key Role of the Principal Student Affairs Officer." Paper presented at the Fifty-Seventh Annual Conference of the National Association of Student Personnel Administrators, San Francisco, March 1975.

CROOKSTON, B. B., and ATKYNS, G. C. "A Study of Student Affairs: The Principal Student Affairs Officer, the Functions, the Organization of American Colleges and Universities 1967–1972 (A Preliminary Summary Report)." Presented at the Forty-Eighth Annual Conference of the National Association of Student Personnel Administrators, Chicago, Illinois, April 15, 1974.

CROOKSTON, B. B., and BLAESSER, W. W. "An Approach to Planned Change in a College Setting." *Personnel and Guidance Journal,* 1962, *40,* 610–616.

CROSS, K. P. "Student Personnel Work as a Profession." *Journal of College Student Personnel,* 1973, *14,* 77–81.

CROSS, K. P. "Assessment of Student Development." Paper presented at the American College Personnel Association Convention, Atlanta, March 1975.

DANSKIN, D. G., and WALTERS, E. D. "Biofeedback and Voluntary Self-Regulation: Counseling and Education." *Personnel and Guidance Journal,* 1973, *51,* 633–638.

DEEGAN, A. X., and FRITZ, R. J. *MBO Goes to College.* Boulder: University of Colorado, 1975.

DELWORTH, U., and AULEPP, L. *Training Manual for Paraprofessionals and Allied Professional Programs.* Boulder: Western Interstate Commission on Higher Education, 1976.

DELWORTH, U., SHERWOOD, G., and CASABURRI, N. *Student Paraprofessionals: A Working Model for Higher Education.* Washington: American College Personnel Association, 1974.

DEWEY, J. *Liberalism and Social Action.* New York: Putnam, 1935.

DRUCKER, P. A. *The Practice of Management.* New York: Harper and Row, 1954.

DUNN, R., and DUNN, K. *Practical Approaches to Individualizing In-*

References

struction: Contracts and Other Effective Teaching Strategies.
New York: Parker, 1972.

Educational Testing Service. *Student Reactions to College,* 1973.

EHRLE, R. A. "Performance Contracting for Human Services." *Personnel and Guidance Journal,* 1970, *49,* 119–122.

EISELE, J. E. "The Counselor and Individualized Instruction." *Personnel and Guidance Journal,* 1973, *52,* 239–244.

ERIKSON, E. H. "Identity and the Life Cycle." In G. S. Klein (Ed.), *Psychosocial Issues.* New York: International Universities Press, 1959.

ERIKSON, E. H. *Childhood and Society.* 2nd ed. New York: Norton, 1963.

ERIKSON, E. H. *Identity: Youth and Crisis.* New York: Norton, 1968.

FELDMAN, K. A., and NEWCOMB, T. M. *The Impact of College on Students.* San Francisco: Jossey-Bass, 1969.

FORDYCE, J. K., and WEIL, R. *Managing with People.* Reading, Mass.: Addison-Wesley, 1971.

FREUD, S. *Civilization and Its Discontents.* New York: Norton, 1930.

FULLMER, D. W., and BERNARD, H. W. *The School Counselor-Consultant.* Boston: Houghton Mifflin, 1972.

GALBRAITH, R., and JONES, T. "Teaching Strategies for Moral Dilemmas: An Application of Kohlberg's Theory of Moral Development to the Social Studies Classroom." *Social Education,* 1975, *39,* 16–22.

GARDNER, J. W. *Self-Renewal.* New York: Harper and Row, 1965.

GARDNER, J. W. "How to Prevent Organizational Dry Rot." *Harper's,* October 1967.

GELATT, H. B., VARENHORST, B., CAREY, R., and MILLER, G. P. *Decisions and Outcomes.* Princeton, N.J.: College Entrance Examination Board, 1973.

GOLDMAN, L. *Using Tests in Counseling.* 2nd ed. New York: Appleton, 1971.

GOLEMBIEWSKI, R. T. *Renewing Organizations.* Itasca, Ill.: Peacock, 1972.

GOSHKO, R. "Self-Determined Behavior Change." *Personnel and Guidance Journal,* 1973, *51,* 629–32.

GOULD, S. B. (Chrmn.), Commission on Non-Traditional Study. *Diversity by Design.* San Francisco: Jossey-Bass, 1973.

GRANT, W. H. "Student Development in the Community College." In T. O'Bannion and A. Thurstone, *Student Development Programs*

References

in the Community Junior College. Englewood Cliffs, N.J.: Prentice-Hall, 1972.

GRANT, W. H. "Humanizing the Residence Hall Environment." In P. A. DeCoster and P. Mable (Eds.), *Student Development and Education in College Residence Halls.* Washington: American College Personnel Association, 1974.

GRONLUND, N. E. *Stating Behavioral Objectives for Classroom Instruction.* New York: Macmillan, 1970.

HALL, B. P. *Value Clarification as Learning Process: A Sourcebook:* New York: Paulist Press, 1973a.

HALL, B. P. *Value Clarification as Learning Process: A Guidebook.* New York: Paulist Press, 1973b.

HARROW, A. J. *A Taxonomy of the Psychomotor Domain.* New York: McKay, 1972.

HARVEY, J. "Administration by Objectives in Student Personnel Programs." *Journal of College Student Personnel,* 1972, *13,* 293–296.

HARVEY, T. R. "Some Future Directions for Student Personnel Administration." *Journal of College Student Personnel,* 1974, *75,* 243–247.

HAVIGHURST, R. J. *Developmental Tasks and Education.* New York: Longman's, 1952.

HAVIGHURST, R. J. *Human Development and Education.* New York: Longman's, 1953.

HAVIGHURST, R. J. "Research on the Developmental Task Concept." *School Review,* 1956, *54,* 215–223.

HEATON, C. P. (Ed.) *Management by Objectives in Higher Education: Theory Cases and Implications.* Durham: National Laboratory for Higher Education, 1975.

HEISLER, V. "Toward a Process Model of Psychological Health." *Journal of Counseling Psychology,* 1961, *11,* 59–62.

HERSHENSON, D. B. "A Functional Organization of College Student Personnel Services," *NASPA Journal,* 1970, *8,* 35–37.

HILL, C. "A Process Approach for Establishing Counseling Goals and Outcomes." *Personnel and Guidance Journal,* 1975, *53,* 571–576.

HILL, J. R. "Human Management Concepts for Student Development Administrators." *Journal of College Student Personnel,* 1974, *15,* 168–170.

HOBERSTROH, C. "Organizational Design and Systems Analysis." In J. A. March (Ed.), *Handbook of Organizations,* Chicago: Rand McNally, 1965.

207

References

HOLLAND, J. L. *Manual for the Vocational Preference Inventory.* 6th rev. ed. Palo Alto, Calif: Consulting Psychologists Press, 1965.

HOLLAND, J. L. *The Self-Directed Search.* Palo Alto, Calif.: Consulting Psychologists Press, 1970.

HOLLAND, J. L. *Making Vocational Choices: A Theory of Careers.* Englewood Cliffs, N.J.: Prentice-Hall, 1973.

HOYT, D. P. "The Impact of Student Personnel Work on Student Development." *NASPA Journal,* 1968, *5,* 269–275.

HURST, J. C., WEIGEL, R. G., MORRILL, W. H., and RICHARDSON, F. C. "Reorganizing for Human Development in Higher Education: Obstacles to Change." *Journal of College Student Personnel,* 1973, *14,* 10–15.

IVEY, A. E. "The Intentional Individual: A Process Outcome View of Behavioral Psychology." *Counseling Psychologist,* 1969, *1,* 59–60.

IVEY, A. E., and ALSCHULER, A. S. (Eds.) "Psychological Education: A Prime Function of the Counselor." *Personnel and Guidance Journal,* 1973, *51,*(9).

IVEY, A. E., and ROLLINS, S. "A Behavioral Objectives Curriculum in Human Relations: A Commitment to Intentionality." *Journal of Teacher Education,* 1972, *23,* 161–165.

JACOB, P. E. *Changing Values in College.* New York: Harper, 1957.

KEIRSEY, D., and BATES, M. *Results Systems Management.* Fullerton: Calif.: Personnel and Guidance Association, 1972.

KERR, C. "Emerging Students and Academic Reform." In *Emerging Students and the New Career Thrust ·in Higher Education.* Iowa City: The American College Testing Program, 1972.

KING, S. H. "The Clinical Assessment of Change." In J. M. Whiteley and H. Z. Sprandel (Eds.), *The Growth and Development of College Students.* Washington: American College Personnel Association, 1970.

KNAPP, J., and SHARON, A. *A Compendium of Assessment Techniques.* Princeton, N.J.: Educational Testing Service, 1975.

KOEHNLINE, W. A. "Learning Clusters: A Creative Alternative." *Community College Frontiers,* 1975, *4,* 27–31.

KOHLBERG, L. "Education for Justice." In J. Gustusson and Others (Eds.), *Moral Education.* Cambridge: Harvard University Press, 1970.

KOHLBERG, L. "Counseling and Counselor Education: A Developmental

References

Approach." *Journal of Counselor Education and Supervision,* 1975, *14,* 250–255.

KOHLBERG, L., and TURIEL, E. *Research in Moral Development: The Cognitive-Developmental Approach.* New York: Holt, Rinehart, and Winston, 1970.

KOHLBERG, L., and TURIEL, E. "Moral Development and Moral Education." In G. Lesser (Ed.), *Psychology and Educational Practice.* Chicago: Scott Foresman, 1971.

KOPPLIN, D. A., and RICE, L. C. "Consulting with Faculty: Necessary and Possible." *Personnel and Guidance Journal,* 1975, *53,* 367–372.

KRAMER, H. "Counselor and Consulting: Using Values in Consultation." *Journal of College Student Personnel,* 1972, *13,* 534–537.

KRATHWOHL, D. R., BLOOM, B. S., and MASIA, B. B. *Taxonomy of Educational Objectives, Handbook II: Affective Domain.* New York: McKay, 1964.

KRUMBOLTZ, J. D. "An Accountability Model for Counseling." *Personnel and Guidance Journal,* 1974, *52,* 639–646.

LANNING, W. "An Expanded View of Consultation for College and University Counseling Centers." *Journal of College Student Personnel,* 1974, *15,* 171–176.

LAUVER, P. J. "Consulting with Teachers: A Systematic Approach." *Personnel and Guidance Journal,* 1974, *52,* 535–540.

LENTON, S. M. "When I Sit and Ask Myself—What's the Role of Student Affairs." Unpublished document. Richmond: Virginia Commonwealth University, 1974.

LEVINE, M. "The Practice of Mental Health Consultation: Some Definitions from Social Theory." in J. Zusman and D. L. Davidson (Eds.), *Practical Aspects of Mental Health Consultation.* Springfield, Ill.: Thomas, 1972.

LEWIN, K. *A Dynamic Theory of Personality.* New York: McGraw-Hill, 1935.

LEWIN, K. *Principles of Typological Psychology.* New York: McGraw-Hill, 1936.

LIKERT, R. *The Human Organization.* New York: McGraw-Hill, 1967.

LIPPITT, R. "Dimensions of the Consultant's Job." *Journal of Social Issues,* 1959, 15, 2, 5–13.

LIPPITT, G. L. *Visualizing Change,* Fairfax, Va.: National Training Laboratories Learning Resources, 1973.

References

LIPPITT, G. L., and SCHMIDT, W. H. "Crises in a Developing Organization." *Harvard Business Review,* 1967, *45,* 102–112.

LOEVINGER, J. *Measuring Ego Development.* San Francisco: Jossey-Bass, 1970.

MAGER, R. F. *Preparing Instructional Objectives.* San Francisco: Fearon, 1962.

MAGER, R. F. *Goal Analysis.* San Francisco: Fearon, 1972.

MASLOW, A. H. *Toward a Psychology of Being.* Princeton, N.J.: Van Nostrand, 1962.

MAYHEW, L. B. Quoted in *Chronicle of Higher Education,* July 22, 1968, pp. 2, 4.

MC ASHAN, H. *The Goals Approach to Performance Objectives.* Philadelphia: Saunders, 1974.

MC BRIDE, A. "Moral Education and the Kohlberg Thesis." *Momentum,* 1973, *4,* 23–27.

MC DANIEL, R. R. "Goal Setting for Student Development." Paper presented at the American College Personnel Association Convention. Atlanta, March 1975.

MC GEHEARTY, L. "The Case for Consultation." *Personnel and Guidance Journal,* 1968, *48,* 355–361.

MILLER, T. K. "Professional Preparation and Development of Residence Educators." In D. A. DeCoster and P. Mable (Eds.), *Student Development and Education in College Residence Halls.* Washington: American College Personnel Association, 1974.

MOORE, M., and DELWORTH, U. *Training Manual for Student Service Program Development.* Boulder: Western Interstate Commission for Higher Education, 1976.

MOOS, R., and GERST, M. *University Residence Environmental Scale Manual.* Palo Alto: Consulting Psychologists Press, 1972.

MORRILL, W. H., OETTING, E. R., and HURST, J. C. "Dimensions of Counselor Functioning." *Personnel and Guidance Journal,* 1974, *52,* 354–359.

MOSHER, R. L., and SPRINTHALL, N. A. "Deliberate Psychological Education." *Counseling Psychologist,* 1971, *2,* 3–82.

MYERS, I., and BRIGGS, K. *Myers-Briggs Type Indicator.* Princeton, N.J.: Educational Testing Service, 1962.

NEWCOMB, T. M. "Student Peer Group Influence and Intellectual Outcomes of College Experience." In R. Sutherland, W. Holtzman,

References

E. Koile, and E. Smith (Eds.), *Personality Factors on the College Campus.* Austin: Hogg Foundations, 1962.

NYE, L. "Obtaining Results Through Modeling." *Personnel and Guidance Journal,* 1973, *51,* 380–384.

ODIORNE, G. S. *Management by Objectives.* New York: Pitman, 1965.

OETTING, E. R., and HAWKES, F. J. "Training Professionals for Evaluative Research." *Personnel and Guidance Journal,* 1974, *52,* 434–438.

OSGOOD, C. E., SUCI, G., and TANNENBAUM, P. H. *The Measurement of Meaning.* Urbana: University of Illinois Press, 1957.

PACE, C. R. *Analyses of a National Sample of College Environments.* Washington: U.S. Department of Health, Education, and Welfare, 1967.

PACE, C. R. *College and University Environment Scales: Technical Manual.* Rev. ed. Princeton, N.J.: Educational Testing Service, 1969.

PACE, C. R., and STERN, G. G. "An Approach to the Measurement of Psychological Characteristics of College Environments." *Journal of Educational Psychology,* 1958, *49,* 269–277.

PARKER, C. A. "Institutional Self-Renewal in Higher Education." *Journal of College Student Personnel,* 1971, *12,* 405–409.

PARKER, C. A. "With An Eye to the Future . . . " *Journal of College Student Personnel,* 1973, *14,* 195–201.

PECK, R. F., and HAVIGHURST, R. J. *The Psychology of Character Development.* New York: Wiley, 1960.

PERRY, W. G., JR. *Forms of Intellectual and Ethical Development in the College Years: A Scheme.* New York: Holt, Rinehart, and Winston, 1970.

PERVIN, L. A. "A Twenty-College Study of Student X College Interaction Using TAPE (Transactional Analysis of Personality and Environment): Rationale, Reliability and Validity." *Journal of Educational Psychology,* 1967, *61,* 281–284.

PERVIN, L. A. "The College as a Social System: Student Perception of Students, Faculty, and Administration." *Journal of Educational Research,* 1968a, *61,* 281–284.

PERVIN, L. A. "Performance and Satisfaction as a Function of Individual-Environment Fit." *Psychological Bulletin,* 1968b, *69,* 56–58.

PETERSON, R. E. *Technical Manual: College Student Questionnaires.*

References

Princeton, N.J.: Educational Testing Service, Institutional Research Program for Higher Education, 1968.

PIAGET, J. *The Origins of Intelligence in Children.* Trans. by McCook. New York: International Universities Press, 1956.

PLOWMAN, P. D. *Behavioral Objectives.* Chicago: Science Research Associates, 1971.

POPPER, K. R. *Conjectures and Reflections: The Growth of Scientific Knowledge.* New York: Harper, 1963.

POWELL, J. R. "In-Service Education for Student Staff." In D. DeCoster and P. Mable (Eds.), *Student Development and Education in College Residence Halls.* Washington: American College Personnel Association, 1974.

PRINCE, J. S. "Identification and Analysis of Selected Developmental Tasks of College Students." Unpublished doctoral dissertation, University of Georgia, 1973.

PRINCE, J. S., MILLER, T. K., and WINSTON, R. B. *Student Developmental Task Inventory Guidelines.* Athens, Ga.: Student Development Associates, 1974.

PRIOR, J. J. "The Reorganization of Student Personnel Services: Facing Reality." *Journal of College Student Personnel,* 1973, *14,* 202–205.

PYRON, T. "The Consultant Role as an Organizational Activity of Student Personnel Workers." *Journal of College Student Personnel,* 1974, *15,* 265–270.

RICE, G., and BISHOPRICK, D. *Conceptual Models of Organizations.* New York: Appleton, 1971.

RIPPY, R. M. *Studies in Transactional Evaluation.* Berkeley, Calif.: McCutchan, 1973.

SANFORD, N. *Self and Society: Social Change and Individual Development.* New York: Atherton, 1966.

SANFORD, N. *Where Colleges Fail.* San Francisco: Jossey-Bass, 1967.

SANFORD, N. "The Goals of Individual Development." In C. Smith (Ed.), *1945–1970: Twenty Five Years of Higher Education.* San Francisco: Jossey-Bass, 1970.

SCHUTZ, W. "FIRO: A Three-Dimensional Theory of Interpersonal Behavior." New York: Holt, Rinehart, and Winston, 1958.

SCRIVEN, M. "The Methodology of Evaluation." *AERA Monograph Series on Curriculum Evaluation,* 1967, No. 1, 39–83.

SHAFFER, R. H. "An Emerging Role of Student Personnel-Contributing

References

to Organizational Effectiveness." *Journal of College Student Personnel,* 1973, *14,* 386–391.

SHEIN, E. H., and BENNIS, W. G. *Personal and Organizational Change Through Group Methods,* New York: Wiley, 1965.

SIMON, S. B. "Values Clarification: A Tool for Counselors." *Personnel and Guidance Journal,* 1973, *51,* 614–619.

SIMON, S. B., HOWE, L. W., and KIRSCHENBAUM, H. *Values Clarification: A Handbook of Practical Strategies for Teachers and Students.* New York: Hart, 1972.

SKINNER, B. F. "Designing Higher Education." *Daedalus,* 1974, *103*(4), 116–202.

SMAIL, M. M., DE YOUNG, A. J., and MOOS, R. H. "The University Residence Environment Scale: A Method for Describing University Student Living Groups." *Journal of College Student Personnel,* 1974, *15,* 357–365.

SPRINTHALL, N. A., and ERICKSON, V. L. "Learning Psychology by Doing Psychology: Guidance Through the Curriculum." *Personnel and Guidance Journal,* 1974, *52,* 397–405.

STANLEY, W. O. *Education and Social Integration.* New York: Teachers College, 1953.

STERN, G. G. *People in Context.* New York: Wiley, 1970.

STIMPSON, R., and SIMON, L. A. K. "Accountability for the Residence Program." In D. A. DeCoster and P. Mable (Eds.), *Student Development and Education in College Residence Halls.* Washington: American College Personnel Association, 1974.

STOYVA, J., and OTHERS (Eds.) *Biofeedback and Self-control.* Chicago: Aldine-Atherton, 1971.

STUFFLEBEAM, D. L. (Chrmn.), Phi Delta Kappa National Study Committee on Evaluation. *Educational Evaluation and Decision-Making.* Itasca, Ill.: Peacock, 1971.

SUPER, D. E., CRITES, J. O., HUMMEL, R. G., MOSER, H. P., OVERSTREET, P. L., and WARNATH, C. F. *Vocational Development: A Framework for Research:* New York: Teachers College, 1957.

SUPER, D. E., STARISHEVSKY, R., MATLIN, R., and JORDAAN, J. P. (Eds.). *Career Development: Self-Concept Theory.* New York: College Entrance Examination Board, 1963.

"Technology in Guidance." *Personnel and Guidance Journal,* 1970, *49*(3).

References

THORESEN, C. E., and MAHONEY, M. J. *Behavioral Self-Control.* New York: Holt, Rinehart and Winston, 1974.

THORNBURG, H. "Adolescence: A Re-interpretation." *Adolescence,* 1970, *20,* 462–484.

TIEDEMAN, D. V., and O'HARA, R. P. *Career Development: Choice and Adjustment.* New York: College Entrance Examination Board, 1963.

TOLLEFSON, A. L. *New Approaches to College Student Development.* New York: Behavioral Publications, 1975.

TREMBLEY, E. L., and BISHOP, J. B. "Counseling Centers and the Issue of Accountability." *Personnel and Guidance Journal,* 1974, *52,* 647–652.

TRYON, C., and LILIENTHAL, J. W. "Developmental Tasks: I. The Concept and Its Importance." In *Fostering Mental Health in Our Schools.* Washington: National Education Assoc., 1950.

TYLER, L. E. *Tests and Measurements.* 2nd ed. Englewood Cliffs, N.J.: Prentice-Hall, 1971.

TYLER, R. W. "Tomorrow's Education." *American Education,* 1975, *11*(7), 16–23.

WALSH, W. B. *Theories of Person-Environment Interaction: Implications for the College Student.* Princeton, N.J.: American College Testing Program, 1973.

WALSH, W. B. "Some Theories of Person/Environment Interaction." *Journal of College Student Personnel,* 1975, *16,* 107–113.

WEINSTEIN, G., and FANTINI, M. D. *Toward Humanistic Education: A Curriculum of Affect.* New York: Praeger, 1970.

WEISBERGER, R. A. *Instructional Process and Media Innovation.* Chicago: Rand McNally, 1968.

Western Interstate Commission for Higher Education. *The Ecosystem Model: Designing Campus Environments.* Boulder, Colo., 1972.

WILLIAMS, R. L., and LONG, J. D. *Toward a Self-Managed Life Style.* Boston: Houghton Mifflin, 1975.

WILLIAMSON, E. G. (Chrmn.), Committee on Student Personnel Work. *The Student Personnel Point of View.* Rev. ed. American Council on Education Studies, Series VI, No. 13. Washington: American Council on Education, 1949.

WISE, L. "Project Talent Eleven Year Follow-Up." Palo Alto, Calif.: American Institutes of Research, 1976.

References

WRENN, C. G. *Student Personnel Work in College,* New York: Ronald, 1951.

YAGER, G. C. "A New Behavioral Emphasis: Turning the Inside Out." *Personnel and Guidance Journal,* 1975, *53,* 585–591.

ZACCARIA, J. S. "Developmental Tasks: Implications for the Goals of Guidance." *Personnel and Guidance Journal,* 1965, *44,* 372–375.

ZUSMAN, J., and DAVIDSON, D. L. (Eds.) *Practical Aspects of Mental Health Consultation.* Springfield, Ill.: Thomas, 1972.

Index

Adolescence, developmental tasks of, 9-10

Adults, young, developmental tasks of, 10-13

ALSCHULER, A. S., 20, 23, 73

Alverno College, 60-61, 129-131, 198

American College Personnel Association (ACPA), xi, 154, 161*n*

American College Testing Program, 116, 140, 141

American Council on Education (ACE), xi, 4, 5

American Institutes for Research, 19

ANASTASI, A., 61

ANDERSON, S. B., 146

Assessment: of affective outcomes, 55-56; application of information from, 61-63; centers and staff for, 69-70; defined, 46-47; environmental, 66-69; examples of, 190-191; information useful in, 53-56; in integrated programs, 174, 178-179, 184; measurement techniques for, 56-61; nature of, 21, 46-71; rationale for, 52-53; remediation contrasted with, 47-48; requirements of, 51-52; stages in process of, 63-66; in student development, 46-71

Assessment measures, 50, 56, 66, 67, 70, 80, 93, 104, 116, 117, 124, 140, 141

ASTIN, A. W., 66, 109

ATKYNS, G. C., 156-157, 159

Auburn University, 100-102, 116-119, 121, 195, 198

AULEPP, L., 69, 105, 124, 132, 141, 146, 166

Austin College, 28-30, 190

AVILA, D. C., 15

Azusa Pacific College, 180-185, 200

216

Index

217

Index

Environment, assessment of, 66-69, 141. *See also* Milieu management
ERICKSON, V. L., 74, 75
ERICKSON, E. H., 6, 7, 10
Evaluation: for accountability, 137-139; defined, 22, 135; examples of, 198-199; goals of, 136-137; for improvement, 143-145; in integrated programs, 175, 179-180, 185; process of, 139-145; reporting of, 144-145; research contrasted with, 135-136; in student development, 134-147

Faculty, 90-92, 155
FANTINI, M. D., 73
Feedback, 59, 61-63
FELDMAN, K. A., 16, 18-19, 111
FORDYCE, J. K., 153
FREUD, S., 6
FRITZ, R. J., 44, 151
FULLMER, D. W., 90

GALBRAITH, R., 15
GARDNER, J. W., 149
GELATT, H. B., 36
Georgia, University of, 94-95, 104-105, 193, 197
GERST, M., 67
Goal setting: application of, 40-42; defined, 21, 27; evaluation of, 141-142; examples of, 189-190; in integrated programs, 174, 178, 184; problems in, 44-45; steps in, 33-36; in student development, 26-45; student development educator's role in, 42-44; training in, 36-40
Goals: defined, 26, 28; individual and program, 27-32; sources of, 32-33; stating of, 33-40
GOLDMAN, L., 61
GOLEMBIEWSKI, R. T., 149
GOSHKO, R., 63
GOULD, S. B., 85
GRANT, W. H., xi, xii, 47, 113, 116, 132
GRONLAND, N. E., 44

HALL, B. P., 58
HARROW, A. J., 18, 44
HARVEY, J., 159-160
HASTINGS, J. T., 55, 64, 143

HAVIGHURST, R. J., 6, 9-10, 15, 20
HAWKES, F. J., 135, 145, 146
HEATON, C. P., 44, 151
HEISLER, V., 112
HERSH, R., 45
HERSHENSON, D. B., 158
Higher education, goals of, 3-4, 169
HILL, C., 59
HILL, J. R., 152
HOBERSTROH, C., 151
HOLLAND, J. L., 66, 110
Hood College, 125-129, 197
Howard University, 103-105, 193
HOYT, D. P., xi, 54
HURST, J. C., 148-149, 162-163, 171
HUXLEY, A., 19

Illinois State University, 68-69, 90-94, 190-196
Instruction: defined, 21-22, 73; examples of, 191-193; implementation of, 85-86; in integrated programs, 75-86, 175, 179, 184; for student development, 72-87; theory of, 74-75
Integration, process of, 18-19. *See also* Programs, integrated
Intellectual development, 14
Intentional student development, 20-25
Iowa State University, 119-121, 197
IVEY, A. E., 20, 23, 73

JACOB, P. E., 18
JONES, T., 15

KAISER, L., 166
KEIRSEY, D., 185
KERR, C., 19
KING, S. H., 8
KNAPP, J., 57, 146
KOEHNLINE, W. A., 179
KOHLBERG, L., 6, 14-15
KRAMER, H., 107
KRATHWOHL, D. R., 18, 44, 55
KRUMBOLTZ, J. D., 137, 144n, 145

LANNING, W., 97-98
LAUVER, P. J., 106
LENTON, S. M., xii, 74
LEWIN, K., 164
LIKERT, R., 44

218